# MORE THAN YOU CAN HANDLE

### WHEN LIFE'S OVERWHELMING PAIN MEETS
### GOD'S OVERCOMING GRACE

## NATE PYLE

ZONDERVAN

*More Than You Can Handle*
Copyright © 2019 by Nathan Pyle

Requests for information should be addressed to:
Zondervan, *3900 Sparks Dr. SE, Grand Rapids, Michigan 49546*

ISBN 978-0-310-34340-0 (softcover)

ISBN 978-0-310-35773-5 (audio)

ISBN 978-0-310-34342-4 (ebook)

Published in association with literary agent Jenni Burke of D.C. Jacobson & Associates LLC, an Author Management Company. www.dcjacobson.com.

*Cover design: Extra Credit Projects*
*Cover photo: ThomasVogel / Getty Images*
*Interior design: Kait Lamphere*

*Printed in the United States of America*

*For Evelyn—*
*the next part of the story is yours to write.*

# CONTENTS

*Foreword by Scott Sauls* ........................... 13

Introduction ...................................... 17

1. More Than You Can Handle................... 23
   *More Darkness Than You Can Handle*

2. Faith Enough to Doubt ..................... 43
   *More Questions Than You Can Handle*

3. How Long, O Lord? ........................ 65
   *More Anger Than You Can Handle*

4. The Deepest Desire......................... 87
   *More Desire Than You Can Handle*

5. Doubting Our Doubts ...................... 107
   *More Faith Than You Can Handle*

6. How Beauty Blooms........................ 127
   *More Mystery Than You Can Handle*

7. Eyes Opened ............................. 147
   *More Empathy Than You Can Handle*

8. Baptism, Crosses, and New Creation.......... 173
   *More Grace Than You Can Handle*

*Acknowledgments*............................. 193
*Notes*....................................... 197

# FOREWORD

Whenever I got upset as a little boy, grown-ups would respond to my loud protests and tears with the standard inquiry, "Scott, what's wrong?"

Since becoming an adult, I have many times asked the same to my own children—as well as to my wife, my friends, my congregants, and anyone else in my world who suffers out loud from the groans of a fallen world.

You seem upset. *What's wrong?*

You seem disappointed. *What's wrong?*

You're crying. *What's wrong?*

I have come to wonder if this question—*What's wrong?*—might be the *wrong* first question to ask a disoriented soul. I'm starting to think that when negative emotions are expressed, the best first question to ask is, *What is right?*

Negative emotion, far from being a wrong emotion, is a God-given release valve, an exhale, a form of protest against a world that's not as it's supposed to be. It is an honest acknowledgment that things have gone sorely wrong. And it is always *right* to act in protest against things that are *wrong*.

Contrary to what we might assume, the Bible is both friend to and champion of negative emotions. Our angst, indignant

13

protests, and gushing tears are woven throughout the pages of the Bible. Standing at the tomb of his friend Lazarus who has been dead for four days, Jesus rages at death and then starts sobbing. The apostle Paul grieves his own covetous heart—*what a wretched man I am!*—and then explains the groan of creation and how famine, nakedness, and sword are the norms of his daily existence. He lives with a thorn in his flesh and begs God to remove it. Jesus does the same at Gethsemane, out of a soul overwhelmed with sorrow, even to the point of death.

Many of the psalms are triggered by experiences that are raw, real, and emotionally charged. In these prayers we find rejoicing, to be sure, but only after the heart has traveled through the valley of the shadow of death, insurmountable sorrow, the agony of betrayal, crushing guilt, and gushing tears. Indeed, these fiercely negative emotions are the breeding ground for some of the most gutsy, honest, and, in the end, *hopeful* prayers ever prayed.

Examine closely the teachings of Jesus, and you'll quickly discover that all the sickness, sorrow, pain, and lament we find there is proof that God hasn't distanced himself at all, but rather is right on time. Far from being signs that God is absent, suffering and sorrow are signs that he is present. Blessed are those who are poor in spirit, who mourn, who hunger and thirst, who are persecuted—for theirs is the kingdom of heaven. It has been granted to us not only to believe in Christ, but also to suffer for his sake.

There is no valley that Jesus asks us to go through that he has not himself gone through first. He entered the abyss all alone so we would never have to be alone. When things go dark for us, he will never leave us or forsake us.

This is the mystery of the gospel and the mystery of grace.

Unless a seed falls to the ground, it abides alone. But when it dies, it bears much fruit. This isn't merely the story of seeds, but the story of life. The story of how things work in a world undergoing renovation. The story of how Jesus, nail by nail and beam by beam, is making all things new.

In retrospect, we are able to see the Story of God better. In his resurrection, Jesus not only overcame death but also paved the way for our sufferings and sorrows to be infused, like his, with infinite meaning.

The renowned grief expert Elisabeth Kübler-Ross wrote, "The most beautiful people we have known are those who have known defeat, known suffering, known struggle, known loss, and have found their way out of the depths."[1]

History, as well as Scripture, demonstrates this to be true. John Bunyan wrote *The Pilgrim's Progress* from prison. Charles Spurgeon dealt with depression all of his adult life. Martin Luther and Martin Luther King Jr. advanced the kingdom, accomplished justice, and kicked darkness in the teeth while simultaneously being opposed and oppressed. Great women like Anne Steele, Fanny Crosby, Sojourner Truth, Harriet Tubman, Amy Carmichael, Elisabeth Elliot, Ann Voskamp, and Joni Eareckson Tada have likewise shaken the earth while facing demons of their own.

These men and women have more than their suffering in common; they are people of Jesus, and they are people of hope. Longing for a better country whose architect and builder is God—a place in which death, mourning, crying, and pain will be no more—they do not lose heart. In Christ, they know that in the ultimate sense their future world is Paradise. It is this future that empowers them to live beautifully in the here and now.

*More Than You Can Handle* is a gift given to us by Pastor Nate Pyle. Its pages tell the story of one whose name can easily be added to those listed above, and of one who pastors his readers through the story of his own pain. With words and anecdotes blending truth, compassion, empathy, he welcomes us into the rapture and rupture of human life—and especially of life in Christ. Nate shepherds us to help us see that, indeed, beautiful lives *can* happen as we surrender to the easy yoke that Jesus has for us.

I hope this book will grant you the courage to face head on the rapture and rupture of your own hopes, dreams, disappointments, and doubts. I hope it will help you feel less alone, less despairing, and more seen and known. I hope it will help you feel more loved, cared for, seen, and *pastored*.

Like all the best pastors do, Nate puts his own life on transparent, vulnerable display and then locates his story inside the gospel itself. In doing so, he paves the way to honest, angsty, gutsy discipleship, which is, of course, the only way into the humble and holy presence of Jesus.

I hope you are as enriched by Nate's words as I have been.

**SCOTT SAULS,**
senior pastor of Christ Presbyterian
Church, Nashville, Tennessee;
author of *Jesus Outside the Lines* and *Irresistible Faith*

# INTRODUCTION

Our guide placed a hand on my shoulder and shook me. "It's time to start walking." I groaned, bemused and bitter about the insanity of his statement. Our watches, phones, and any other electronic device capable of tracking the time of day were taken from us at the beginning of the trip, so there was no way to know exactly what time it was. I didn't need a watch to know the time was ungodly. The heavy blanket of dark covering everything and the frost on my sleeping bag told me all I needed to know.

It was not time to wake up.

But he didn't tell us to wake up. He only said it was time to start walking.

Once camp had been stuffed into our backpacks and the sleep unsuccessfully rubbed from our eyes, we trudged single file forward into the dark. Not just any kind of dark, but the kind of dark you can *feel*. The kind your eyes push against, as if the darkness were a wall that could be pushed over if only your eyes could strain a little harder. But with the dark, there's nothing to push against. Darkness isn't an object you can move; it's only an absence you can fill. Into it we walked.

Despite being intangible, there is a sense in which darkness seems to have object-like qualities. It can be oppressive.

Fear inducing. Or to some (or perhaps to all, depending on the situation), a form of protection, like a blanket to hide under.

Darkness has the ability to separate those who are standing close. Darkness breeds loneliness. Two people can be within inches of each other, sharing the same space, breathing the same air, dreaming the same dreams and yet utterly disconnected, as though the lightless barrier were an impassable gorge. Maybe this is why we're scared of the dark.

Or maybe we're scared of no longer being able to see—see both what we're facing and whether anyone is with us. We know that if we weren't alone, we'd be able to face the uncertain with more courage, but the inability to see others increases our sense of loneliness.

That loneliness compounds our fears. We become scared to find out what would happen if we switched on the light. Are we more alone than we thought?

Or maybe the darkness is our hiding place. Our real fear is being seen—really seen. And so we choose to hide in the dark, lonely as it may be.

That night—or morning, if we want to be technical—the sky seemed utterly void of light. We were in a thick forest at the bottom of a small canyon, and any light that might have been above us was blocked by a ceiling of leaves.

I'm not sure how long we hiked. A while. The students on the trip were complaining of the cold, but our guides wouldn't let them put on more clothes. Add too many clothes on a chilly morning, and with a bit of sweat, you run the risk of overheating. I sighed quietly so the students couldn't hear me. I took the admonition against extra clothing to mean we would be walking for quite a while more. Uphill. I'm not afraid of the dark, but this much dark was unsettling. The darkness embodied the uncertainty of why we were walking and where we were walking to. It would be nice to see the sun start to push back the darkness. At least we would be able to see a bit farther in front of our feet.

The trail began to rise gradually and then, like it does in the mountains, much more steadily. The higher we went, the more stars we could see. One by one, constellation by constellation, stars became visible through the trees if only we had looked up. After hours of walking with little sleep and a heavy pack, most of us had our heads down, headlamps illuminating the trail just in front of our feet, and didn't notice what was unfolding above us. We crested the top of a ridge and found ourselves on a plateau of sorts—a vast, barren mountain ridge above the tree line.

"Turn off your headlamps and look at the sky," our guide said.

Looking up, I saw the most expansive nighttime sky I've ever seen—stars and galaxies from horizon to horizon—an expanse that stretched farther than normal, because when you're on top of a mountain, you get to look down on the horizon. The thin mountain air provided less resistance for the starlight, and all of us—three adults and nine high school students—stood in awe at the sheer number of stars. It seemed like we were looking up at the blackest paper imaginable—a paper protecting us from a light so bright that it would have blinded us more than the darkness, dotted with pinholes allowing us to get a glimpse of the brightness behind it.

The Milky Way was like a giant shimmering scar across the face of the sky. Constellations came alive. Ursa Major grazed in the heavenly meadow alongside the she-bear Ursa Minor; Draco flew in his serpentine manner around the stars; Cepheus and Cassiopeia watched and ruled over it all.

The darkness could not extinguish the beauty. In fact,

because of the darkness, the stars shone more brightly. Looking at the early morning sky, I noticed that Orion, the hunter, my favorite constellation, was missing. I scanned the sky; he should have been so bright! Was he over the horizon?

Then I remembered that it was July. At this time of the year, Orion is in the sky during the day, its faint light imperceptible against the bright sun.

You see, some things only shine when it's dark.

Written on the barracks wall of Auschwitz is a poem scrawled by an anonymous inmate:

> There is grace, though,
> and wonder, on the way.
> Only they are hard to see,
> hard to embrace, for
> those compelled to
> wander in the darkness.[1]

This is a book about finding God and grace as we wander in a darkness that is more than we can handle. It's about the moments when we're so overwhelmed that we wander directionless toward unknown destinations. It's about those times when we wonder if the God who promises to guide us has run far ahead and left us behind to stumble in the darkness on our own.

I don't claim to be an expert on suffering. I definitely wouldn't claim that my suffering is greater than others. I've found that comparing pain is a futile endeavor that robs us of our humanity; it replaces compassion with competition, empathy with callousness. But I've wandered in my own darkness and been invited into the darkness of others enough to have learned a few things.

First, I've learned that we can't avoid suffering. It's going to happen. And we'll never know how we will respond to pain and tragedy until we go through it. In fact, the moments of wondering and wandering don't just happen. In many ways, they have to happen. They have to happen because we're human. We can't be anything else. We can't be omnipotent and omniscient. We can't be impenetrable and unmovable. However, we can pretend. We can power through. We can close off our emotions. But these things don't change the fact that we'll always be vulnerable.

Suffering is the universal human experience that unites all of us. To be human is to suffer. On the one hand, this is a tragic condition; on the other hand, perhaps it is hopeful. For suffering also turns over the soil of our souls, readying them for something new.

Second, any explanation for suffering is unlikely to be found in the pages that follow. That's a bitter pill to swallow, but accepting the fact that our questions will go unanswered seems necessary to finding the light in the darkness. Please hear me: this doesn't mean our questions shouldn't be asked. We must ask them if we are going to bring all of who we are to all of who God is. Not only that, it's through our questions that a new kind of relationship is forged. But that still doesn't mean we'll get answers. Only that there is space for questions.

Third, we never wander in the darkness alone, no matter what we think.

I'm sure there's more learning I could share, and some will be shared over the course of the book. But I know these three things are true. They're a good place to start. From here, we'll wander in the dark together and, hopefully, embrace a grace and wonder that's more than we can handle.

# CHAPTER 1

# MORE THAN YOU CAN HANDLE

## More Darkness Than You Can Handle

> The journey has to feel like night because it leads into the unknown . . . If Christianity meant mere maintenance, then bewilderment or darkness would spell disaster. But if there really is somewhere to go, then darkness, the flip-side of the unfamiliar, is a condition of Christian life.
>
> Iain Matthew, *The Impact of God*

The Good Book says the Lord is close to the brokenhearted,[1] which leaves me wondering if he ever comes to the suburbs. The neighborhoods—with streets lined by Bradford pear trees whose branches, blowing gently in the wind, salute the weary returning from work to their manicured lawns, freshly painted houses, matching mailboxes, and children circling cul-de-sacs on shiny bikes—give off the appearance of a carefully fashioned Eden. We pretend that with enough spit and polish, decay can be thwarted. Homeowner's associations craft regulations to ensure that mailboxes are replaced when worn, cars are kept off the street, lawns are uncluttered, and house colors are chosen from the same palette for a pleasing neighborhood aesthetic. Convenience, safety, and comfort drive the impulses of the quintessential American neighborhood. Nothing is old. Nothing without purpose. Nothing broken. And what does break is quickly discarded and replaced. So intoxicating is the pursuit of our self-made Eden that, if possible, I'm sure we'd trade in our hearts for ones that don't bruise, lest we ruin the facade.

But life isn't a well-protected garden. And sometimes you can't keep the ruse going any longer.

Much of my life has been suburban. My cracks and broken-ness were buried behind a well-kept exterior. I smiled when I was sad, played the extrovert when I was lonely, and stuck my chest out with manufactured bravado when I was scared. But life has a funny way of dealing with our pretense. At some point, we find ourselves like the little Dutch boy. Our trusty dam that has long held back the waters of life—financial security, a solid marriage, a successful career, even religion—is riddled with cracks from life's pressure. So we jam our fingers into the widening cracks that are spider-webbing across our cheap dam, frantically trying to save our lives. But eventually the cracks outnumber our fingers and are more than we can handle. The water bursts through the dam, and we're swept away like a tiny leaf in a strong current.

It reminds me of a story Jesus once told.[2] Two men built houses. One built his house on the sand, and the other built his house on the rock. After the two men moved into their homes, a storm began. The winds blew, fatiguing the houses. Torrent after torrent of rain wooed the streams over their banks, creating a malevolent, swirling mess that washed away the house built on the sand. I remember singing the song that went along with this story when I was in Sunday school.[3] The message I inter-nalized was simple: when you build your life upon the Rock, Jesus, nothing will harm you. Which meant that anytime I was harmed—being mocked mercilessly in middle school, getting into a bad car accident, my engagement falling apart, being fired from my youth pastor job—I assumed my faith was inadequate in some way. I must not have trusted God enough. I failed to pray enough, read my Bible enough, evangelize enough.

Maybe you've felt this way too.

Never enough.

Every bad experience shared this theoretical common denominator. Never enough.

*Not smart enough.*

*Not prepared enough.*

*Not strong enough.*

*Not liked enough.*

*Not courageous enough.*

*Not connected enough.*

*Not enough faith.*

*Not enough.*

Sometimes we suffer the consequences of our actions. But not always. Truth is, whether your house is built on the sand or on the rocks, at some point everyone tastes the rain mixing with tears while winds threaten to knock down our fragile houses. Whether we acknowledge what threatens us is another question. Too many of us quietly trudge through our trials. Staying up late, sitting at the kitchen table under the glow of a single light, we wonder if that light will be on in two weeks because we haven't paid the bill. Holding a screaming baby for yet another sleepless night, feeling guilty that being a mother hasn't been an experience filled with joy. There aren't hashtags for these situations. They aren't public. In fact, many of us would consider our pain minor in the face of other people's suffering. "It's not that bad," we say. "I have it better than most," we rationalize. But comparison is a game the house always wins.

If you haven't heard it before, let me be the first to say it—or if you've heard it before—let me remind you: Your pain is real. Your suffering is legitimate. What you are facing is more than you can handle.

In 2 Corinthians 4:7, Paul refers to humans as clay jars, and I think he's onto something. On the one hand, our strength comes because we've been forged in fire. On the other hand, we still chip. We get pressed on every side. Cracks threaten our integrity. What's inside bleeds out into the world. No one is immune from this part of the human experience. If it hasn't happened to you, it will. And if it has happened to you, if you've felt your heart bursting and bleeding and losing its ability to contain the pain and fear, then you know: life is often more than you can handle.

This isn't theory for me. I know this. I've been overwhelmed by life too.

■  ▨  ▨

It was March 2013. My wife and I had been struggling to get pregnant for more than a year. Again.

Conceiving our first child took us fourteen months. I clearly remember the day we found out she was pregnant—July 4. Friends were visiting from California, and on the morning they planned to leave, my wife woke me up by jumping on the bed next to me. I jerked awake and gave her a confused and slightly angry look.

"What are you doing?" I grunted.

She lay next to me and drew her mouth close to my ear. Whispering, she said, "I'm pregnant."

I jolted up. "What!" I exclaimed at the risk of waking our guests. "No you're not!"

But I believed her. The look on her face. The unforced joy in her smile. The dancing of her eyes. The sweetness of her voice. It all convinced me. This was no lie. Our prayers were answered, and now we were going to go say good morning to our guests while keeping a secret that required every ounce of restraint we possessed.

The second time we tried to become pregnant was very different.

Our first pregnancy taught us that conceiving a child wasn't a simple science experiment. Meticulously following the right steps in the right order doesn't necessarily yield the desired result. Based on this experience, we prepared ourselves to wait for our second child. Fourteen months came and went. Fifteen months. Eighteen months. Two years. We were finding ourselves on a roller coaster we hadn't been prepared to ride. Unlike most roller coasters, this one didn't last minutes. We measured its duration in days—twenty-eight to be exact. Everyone who has struggled with infertility despises the jolting ups and downs— hope, discouragement, hope, frustration, hope, despair. It's a ride you never get to exit. At the end of twenty-eight days, we'd climb back up the hill of hope, only to be flung back down. We never gave up hope, and we were never numb to the pain of disappointment. Every month hurt with increasing volume.

On top of that, it had been a trying season because of revelations that shook a ministry I was deeply involved in. A good friend, who had founded the ministry, had been caught in an adulterous relationship with a woman. I knew the implications his affair would have would be serious, but I didn't know that within months of this discovery, the ministry would effectively be dismantled.

So I was already emotionally exhausted when the monthly roller-coaster ride began to last longer.

Twenty-nine days. Thirty days. My excitement grew, but I didn't talk about it, just like a pitcher doesn't talk about throwing a no-hitter in the seventh inning. When I finally broke and dared to say something, it was clear my wife didn't share my optimism.

"It just feels different," she stated flatly.

Thirty-one days.

At this point, she took the test.

I waited in the other room.

She came out, but her eyes didn't dance.

My heart dropped. "No?"

"It says I'm pregnant."

"Then what's the problem? Why aren't you more excited?"

"Something . . . isn't right. I can't tell what it is, but it's not right."

"We've got to wait and see what the doctor says," I said to comfort her. In retrospect, I probably said it to soothe my own anxiety. I saw her eyes. "We should celebrate until we hear otherwise."

As confident as I tried to be, there was a chink in my armor. Sarah is usually right about this kind of stuff. She has an uncanny intuition that can be downright scary.

Sarah called the doctor's office and made an appointment. Within a day or so, she went in to get blood work done in order to confirm the pregnancy. So far, so good.

We got a call when the results came back. One of the hormone levels was low, and the doctor wanted to have an ultrasound done right away. Now we were concerned. What could an ultrasound possibly show this early in the pregnancy?

Ultrasound rooms are usually tiny and sparsely decorated but never barren. Despite having enough space to contain a couple, the examination chair, a technician, and clinical equipment, they are pregnant with emotions. They are usually painted some kind of muted tone of beige, with a nondescript picture of a potted plant or a print of Anne Geddes hanging on the wall.

Yet one doesn't have a mundane experience in an ultrasound room. It isn't like taking your car in for a tire rotation. Your time in that room is marked with extreme joy or profound sadness. There are only highs and lows, no ho hums. We understood this, and we weren't sure what our time in the room would mean. So we carried in a tightly wound ball of anxiety, and without any place to set it, we let the ball settle into our stomachs.

I held Sarah's hand. The technician prepared the transducer probe. An image appeared on the TV screen, and we sat in silence. Desperately, we searched the grainy image for anything that made sense to us—a small ball of orangish light fluttering, a clear depiction of something implanted in the uterine wall. Anything that would say, "Everything is okay."

My eyes darted back and forth between the screen and the technician's face. Maybe I'd catch a glimpse of something that would give me an indication. The slightest upturning of the corner of her mouth. A heartbeat. A brief scowl. A little lima bean at the center of the screen. A little extra wetness in the eyes.

Nothing.

Stoically, the technician flipped off the machine and handed Sarah a towel.

"When you're ready, come out and the doctor will see you."

The door closed and the tears began. Despite the lack of evidence, we sensed that whatever was coming, it wasn't going to be good.

We made our way to the next sterile room. After a short wait, the doctor arrived. Briskly he came in and sat on a stool. His greeting wasn't as warm as it usually was. He lacked the poker face of his technician. The corners of his mouth were taut. His face was weighed down by an unfamiliar gravity. It confirmed our fears.

Getting straight to the point, he told us that between the hormone levels and the ultrasound, the pregnancy was likely ectopic. This meant the embryo hadn't made it all the way to the uterus and was lodged somewhere in a Fallopian tube. My heart sank. I squinted to try to stay focused on what he was saying.

The doctor compassionately explained our options. The first was a simple shot that would chemically end the pregnancy. It was so simple that we could do it before we left the hospital. Hope, possibility, life—terminated with a simple shot. The second option was to wait and hope his suspicions were wrong. It meant risking a possible ruptured Fallopian tube, surgery, and, if not treated soon enough, infection and possibly death.

"Are you sure this pregnancy is ectopic?" Sarah asked.

"No," the doctor answered slowly. "There is no way to be certain this early in the pregnancy. We can only make an educated guess based on the tests and the ultrasound."

"So you're asking us to consider ending a pregnancy on a guess?" I nearly whispered. I was having difficulty trying to wrap my mind around what was happening.

Between our convictions that even if this embryo wasn't in the uterus, it was a child who bore the image of God, and the shock of the situation, we were spiraling in a vortex of questions.

What if things were just taking their sweet time getting rolling? What if the fetus was in the uterus? How do you make a decision of this magnitude on a guess? How much of a risk would we put Sarah in if we waited? If the Fallopian tube ruptured, would that lessen our chance of future kids? How can we think about future children when there's still this child? Is there a possibility that the embryo could make its way to the uterus? Could God's hand pluck it from its current location and place it where it belongs? Could we live with ending what could be a viable pregnancy?

We couldn't.

After much conversation, we decided we were willing to take a bit of a risk and wait. We weren't going to do anything, and we'd come back in a week to check on things. After all our praying and waiting, we couldn't end the pregnancy now.

As we drove away from the doctor's office, I called my parents. This was Tuesday. On Friday we were all scheduled to fly to Colorado to celebrate their sixtieth birthdays with a ski trip (their birthdays are twelve days apart). We had to back out of the trip in order to keep Sarah close to the hospital in case something happened.

Sarah cried in the seat next to me as I talked with my parents. I hung up the phone, and Sarah looked at me and, through red, teary eyes, apologized.

"I'm so sorry."

"What could you possibly have to apologize for?" I was incredulous that she would be apologizing.

"This is my fault. It's my body. It doesn't work the way it's supposed to."

It is absurd what we believe when life gets brutal. Lies that were planted years before through incidents—good and bad—and words come into full bloom when fertilized with the dung of life.

I grabbed her hand, looked directly in her eyes, and assured her, "You have nothing to apologize for."

She knew that. On a cognitive level, we all know we don't cause every trial we face. But there are times when it seems easier to believe we are the cause. That somehow we are to blame, or even that we deserve whatever trial we encounter. And the fact that, at that moment, I couldn't convince her that this was a lie was cruel. As if the emotional and physical trauma weren't already enough, being dealt feelings of shame on top of everything else seemed especially unfair.

I didn't feel it then, but a darkness crept up on me there in the car. It seethed and pulsed like the constant hum of fluorescent lights. It never scared me. It was simply present, like a dull muscle ache pulling with a constant tension. I couldn't see what exactly it was, but I see it now.

Anger.

There I was—feeling betrayed by a friend's indiscretions, frustrated that we were missing a trip with my family and not being able to be present for my parents' birthday celebrations, all the while trying to wrap my mind around the possibility of ending a pregnancy we so desperately wanted. I always thought my house was built on the rock, but this storm made it feel like the sand was washing out from under me.

So I did the only thing I had energy for. I wept.

■ ■ ■

"God won't give you more than you can handle."

That's one of the most common axioms we are handed in the midst of intense grief. Well intentioned, sure. Everyone needs to be encouraged, and what better way than by letting someone know they must be strong enough to face whatever circumstance lies before them because the Divine has deemed them able. But for all its well-meaning consolation, it's about as scriptural as "God helps those who help themselves," and "Cleanliness is next to godliness." Which is to say, it's not. You can make the argument for these sentiments using the Bible, but you have to be a trained contortionist to make everything bend the right way.

The support for "God won't give you more than you can handle" comes from 1 Corinthians 10:13, where Paul writes, "God is faithful; he will not let you be *tempted* beyond what you can bear" (emphasis added). Notice that the verse is about temptation. It's not about being overwhelmed by life. This verse wasn't intended to be a comfort to someone reeling from the loss of a child. Paul wasn't meaning for someone to rely on their own strength while fighting cancer. God didn't take away your job so you could see how strong you are.

Far too often, interpretations of Scripture that make sense when life is generally comfortable are taken as true. But if the interpretation only works in the suburbs, where our lawns are trimmed and our pretenses are secured like vinyl siding, then it's probably safe to assume that the interpretation doesn't work. Apply the idea that God won't give you more than you can handle to other situations, and it's blatantly obvious that this idea only works in relatively benign situations.

To a survivor of Auschwitz say, "God won't give you more than you can handle."

To a young girl sold into prostitution say, "God won't give you more than you can handle."

To a Christian in Iraq whose world has been destroyed by ISIS say, "God won't give you more than you can handle."

To a mother who lost her daughter to a Palestinian bomber say, "God won't give you more than you can handle."

To a father from the poverty-stricken countryside of Cambodia who was injured while hunting for food and can no longer work and provide for his family say, "God won't give you more than you handle."

Seems cold, even heartless, no? A tone-deaf response imploring good ole American "pull yourself up by your boot-straps" theology to situations involving people understandably overwhelmed by a brutal world. It doesn't offer help but merely provides the speaker an opportunity to not get involved—to distance themselves from any responsibility. There's no need to help because they should be able to handle it. And to the one suffering, this phrase says, *Please don't ask for help because you should be able to handle whatever it is you're going through, because God in his divine omniscience gave it to you.*

One can't help but wonder if the phrase isn't more for the person who offers it as misguided comfort. Seeing others suffer shakes our confidence in human durability and embarrasses us. A kind of survivor's guilt washes over us as we thank the Lord for our well-being when confronted with another's adversity. We feel that we should help them, while at the same time we feel guilty because of our packed schedules. Overwhelmed by the suffering in front of us, we distance ourselves from it in order to relieve our discomfort.

Coming into contact with the ill and broken reminds us of our own helplessness and susceptibility to suffering. We could lose our jobs. Our spouse could cheat on us. The hope we have for our kids' future could be erased by heroin. And we wonder, *If that happens, can I handle it?* So we spout the phrase to those who are actually walking through life's valleys, hoping that if they can handle it, we might be able to handle it too.

Truth is, none of us can really handle life. There's too much joy, too much sorrow, too much beauty, too much pain. Life—with its baby giggles, courageous cancer survivors, immense poverty, brutal trafficking of young girls, and redemptive stories of justice—is paralyzingly large. Those who say they can manage real life aren't paying attention to the fathomless ocean of human emotion.

Implying that we can handle whatever storm threatens our house is not biblical. If anything, it is the exact opposite. Look at what Paul writes in 2 Corinthians 1:8–9:

> We do not want you to be uninformed, brothers and sisters, about the troubles we experienced in the province of Asia. We were under great pressure, far beyond our ability to endure, so that *we despaired of life itself.* Indeed, we felt we had received the sentence of death. But *this happened that we might not rely on ourselves but on God*, who raises the dead (emphasis mine).

Paul—the one who was shipwrecked for the sake of the gospel, whose faith was so strong that people were healed when they touched rags he used to wipe his brow, who converted guards while in jail, who brazenly stood before rulers and confessed Jesus as Lord—said he despaired of life. He didn't just have a bad day. You don't despair of life after the flu or getting cut off in traffic or when your kids talk back to you. No, this pillar of faith thought life was too much. The pain was too great. He wanted to give up. He considered abandoning everything because it no longer seemed worth the struggle. He probably felt like a failure.

But later in the same letter, Paul would write, "When I am weak, then I am strong" (2 Corinthians 12:10). It is when we are at our frailest that Christ's power can rest on us (see verse 9). In other words, when we can no longer keep going. When we're fed up. When we're empty. Confused. Exhausted. In over our heads. When life is too much to handle. In those moments, the strength of Christ's resurrection will be seen in us. This is gospel news. This is *good* news.

But it is also bad news. The unfortunate thing about resurrection is that it can only be experienced after death. Until we die, we think we can do something to bring life to our weary bodies. But we need the God of death and resurrection to come into our broken lives, dead dreams, and hopeless situations. That's what Good Friday and Easter are about. Jesus enters our death so that, with him, we might be given new life. If we want to experience this resurrection, then we must stop trying to perform CPR on our lives. As C. S. Lewis said at the very end of his classic book *Mere Christianity*, "Nothing in you that has not died will ever be raised from the dead."[4]

Death teaches this cruel fact: I can't handle everything. Neither can you.

But that's okay. Because that's where God will meet us.

■　■　■

The searing pain and bleeding started Saturday night. We called the doctor and were told to head to the emergency room right away. We left our son, Luke, with Sarah's parents, who were in town just in case we had to take Sarah to the hospital if something were to go wrong. We got in the car. I held her hand as we drove in silence. There was nothing to say. We knew what this meant and what was going to happen.

Sarah softly cried.

I kept holding her hand, fixing my eyes on the road, focused on getting to the hospital, but desperately trying to figure out what I could say that would fix this situation. Something that would offer an explanation to make sense of it.

After we checked in at the emergency room, we were pointed to a room filled with muted yellow chairs where we could sit and wait until our name was called. An ectopic pregnancy can in some cases cause the Fallopian tubes to explode. It sounded urgent to us, and yet we sat, just like everyone else in the emergency room, engaged in bitter speculation about the true condition of those whose condition the triage team had determined was more dire than ours.

I had never felt more helpless. I wanted to stand up and scream, but all I could manage was to bounce my leg in nervous protest. This entire ordeal handcuffed my predisposition to do something. I can't sit idly by. I need to get into action and take control. When the dishwasher breaks, I attempt to repair it. When the computer is on the fritz, I will hack my way through operating systems, blindly deleting the files Google tells me I don't need. If there is ambiguity about what's going to happen Friday night, I coordinate an effort to solidify plans. My drive to fix situations and things is nearly obsessive. I'll perseverate on a problem until it's resolved. But sitting on that yellow chair was the most I could do. In that moment, in that situation, there was no other action to take. I couldn't mend our infertility. I couldn't usher the child into Sarah's uterus. There was nothing I could correct. I could only wait.

Eventually, our names were called, and we made our way past all the others who were clearly questioning the state of our emergency. We went into a room that lacked an Anne Geddes on the wall. There was no calming music playing. All that filled the room were tools necessary for attending to medical emergencies and the sound of medical machines beeping from neighboring rooms. After reviewing our chart, another ultrasound was ordered. Sarah was wheeled through the emergency room, and we carried that same ball of anxiety into another small, cramped ultrasound room.

I held my breath when the image flashed on the screen. It didn't take long to see it—a small, bluish-white dot along a long line. I didn't have a degree in radiology, but I knew this was the last time I would see this child.

At this point in the story, I realize there may be some people who take offense with my use of *child* in reference to what some would call a ball of cells. But I don't know what else to call it. I've felt the temptation to call it a blastocyst or even an embryo. Technical terms make it easier to distance yourself from the pain of loss. But how do you distance yourself from something you've labored in prayer over? I don't know. I'm still at a loss as to what to refer to this as. But *child* seems fitting, because wrapped up with pregnancy is possibility and hope, and that's exactly what had been bound to this child.

After we returned to the emergency room, we waited for what seemed like an eternity. Close to midnight, the doctor came into the room and confirmed our fears. The pregnancy was ectopic, and we would have to end it.

"Lucky for you all, it is early enough in the pregnancy that we don't have to do surgery. We can simply do this with a shot," he said.

*Lucky.*

The shot would essentially roll back the pregnancy. When a sperm and egg unite, they form a zygote after the initial cell division. One cell becomes two. Two becomes four. Four becomes sixteen. Mitosis begets rapid growth as the embryo makes its way to the uterus. This shot is meant to stop the growth and then slowly reverse the process. Thirty-two becomes sixteen. Sixteen becomes eight. Eight becomes four. Four becomes two. Two becomes one. The ball of cells gets smaller and smaller and smaller until the woman's body becomes a grave for the misplaced life.

Sarah sat on the medical table, and I stood next to her. We both closed our eyes and wept.

We didn't watch the needle. Sarah barely winced when it pierced her skin.

We were both crying. The pain was intense, but it wasn't coming from the needle.

■  ■  ■

When life is more than we can handle, everything feels out of control. The book of Genesis begins with a chaotic darkness that hovers over the unformed world. The formlessness of the universe rages like the turbulent waters of a stormy sea. Whatever elements and particles are caught in the violent vortex crash together haphazardly, creating more chaos. The Hebrew phrase describing this dark chaos is *tohu wabohu*. It's the Hebrew equivalent of *helter-skelter.* Even the phrase itself, *tohu wabohu,* has a dizzying reduplication of sounds. With *tohu wabohu,* there is no structure. There is no organization. There is no heaven and earth. There is no distinction between land and sea. There is no separation of light and dark. In the unformed world, darkness knows no boundary, but it oppresses the universe with its unrelenting bedlam.

Sometimes I wonder if our world has progressed much beyond the *tohu wabohu.* It often seems as though we have entered a great reversal—a return of sorts to disorder and darkness. Our news feeds are filled with horrific acts of wickedness that turn our stomachs. Social media has made the dark chaos seem more omnipresent than ever. Hashtag after hashtag reminds us of the brokenness: #BlackLivesMatter. #ICantBreathe. #BringBackOurGirls. #PrayForParis. #PrayForBrussels. #RefugeesWelcome. #SandraBland. #KalamazooShooting. #ISIS. #Aleppo. #Charlottesville. #MeToo. And scattered among these major societal concerns are countless individual tragedies.

Not long ago, our city was shaken by the story of a young mother who was murdered after three men randomly entered her home. What shocked us was how arbitrary it was. These men didn't know her. They walked down a street and picked a house. That's it. No planning. No forethought. Just an aimless crime. A lottery pick of violence.

Unfortunately, this isn't a unique, random event.

We all have stories like this. Stories that cause us to shake our heads in bewilderment. Stories that make us wonder if there is any divine involvement in this world. Stories that, if we are being honest, make us a little more afraid and a little more likely to double-check the locks on our doors at night. Some of us are living this story.

For all our efforts, we cannot tame the crashing together

of the universe's particles and subdue the chaos. It's why life often feels unwieldy. In response, we prepare and plan for every possible tragedy—buy insurance, not let our kids out of our sight, buckle our seat belts, and wear bike helmets. But we can't ever plan for the event that comes at us sideways. It always catches us off guard, knocking the wind out of our chests and dropping us to our knees. Science will never solve the problem of pain. Fortune tellers will never prepare us. We, on the inside, cannot fix this; we need someone from outside to rescue us.

In Genesis, we find the Spirit of God hovering over the waters of chaos. God's creative act reigns in the *tohu wabohu*. Life isn't an accident, but it exists because of the purpose of God, who orders the chaos. Out of his great love, God separates the light from the darkness, bringing order and beauty and purpose to the creation.

After creation, a new kind of darkness enters the creation. Sin ruptured Eden, returning chaos to order, discord to peace, *Sheol* to *shalom*. Thorns and thistles sprang up from the ground and grew into our lives. We tasted tears and death for the first time. Suffering is the consequence of sin. While not all trials are a direct result of our personal sin, senseless trials are a consequence of a broken, sin-filled world.

John's gospel offers an additional image—one that changes everything. The One who created the universe, who tamed its stormy waters, not only tames the darkness but enters the darkness. Jesus sustains creation by holding back the chaos. Jesus walks on the stormy waters.[5] Jesus commands the turbulent winds to be quiet.[6]

To paraphrase John, for God so loved this messed-up, chaotic world that he sent his Son, Jesus, into the helter-skelter.[7]

And into your helter-skelter.

# CHAPTER 2

# FAITH ENOUGH TO DOUBT
## *More Questions Than You Can Handle*

I think there is no suffering greater than what is caused by the doubts of those who want to believe. I know what torment this is, but I can only see it, in myself anyway, as the process by which faith is deepened. A faith that just accepts is a child's faith and all right for children, but eventually you have to grow religiously as every other way, though some never do.

Flannery O'Connor, *The Habit of Being*

ancer occupied much of Bernice's body by the time I met her. She was a sweet, short Midwestern woman whose age caught everyone off guard because of her vitality. Her tidy house was sparsely decorated. Her minimalism was by circumstance, not choice. Despite being just beyond seventy and having her body invaded by cancer, Bernice's self-sufficient pride kept her working to provide for her daughter and grandson after her daughter's messy divorce. Supporting them left her with little for herself.

The few things she did have were neatly placed around the house. The particleboard television cabinet with a faux oak finish was centered on the one non-windowed wall in the living room. On top of the cabinet were a handful of Precious Moments figurines, looking at one another across the vast, otherwise empty expanse. The living room was spacious, or at least it appeared that way since there was only a couch and an Amish-style rocking chair in the room. A single, framed cross-stitched picture of a watering can acting as a flowerpot adorned the wall opposite the couch.

She offered me a seat on her couch and then sat across from me in the rocking chair. Her feet barely reached the floor as she rocked herself by pushing on the floor with her toes. Evidence of chemo treatments were plain to see, but Bernice worked to draw attention away from them. She wore a colorful bandana to cover her chemo-scorched hair. Her bright smile provided color to her otherwise ashen skin. Bernice was tenacious about her appearance and refused to play the part of the cancer patient. One couldn't help but like her.

I began our conversation with simple pleasantries. Bernice wasn't having it. This was a woman who preferred to talk about what was really on her mind.

"God's gonna heal me, pastor," she began. "I just know it."

The force of her conviction caught me off guard. Bernice had stage 4 lung cancer that wasn't confined to her lungs. According to the doctors, she was terminally ill. According to her, she was a miracle in process.

"I have faith. That's what we have to have, right? No room for doubting the Lord's goodness. If you believe, he'll heal you. I heard a pastor say that last night on the television. In fact, I'm going to Ohio in a couple of weeks to see a faith healer."

The cancer was far enough along that the three-hour drive was too difficult for her to do alone. So a friend was going to drive her to Cincinnati, where they would attend a faith healer's revival. The setting for this night of miracles would be a hotel conference room. Her plan was straightforward, her goals simple—attend the revival, get healed, enjoy her restored body, get back to work, and help her daughter and grandson get their lives back together. She'd be able to make it back to church more regularly and start helping others. She wouldn't need people looking after her. She would once again contribute to the world around her. She'd grow her own hair again.

What Bernice lacked in material possessions she made up for in optimism, hard work, and tenacity. All of this made me wonder, *How much of her attitude is necessity and how much is natural disposition?*

Having just come from our Sunday worship service, I was still wearing my Sunday clothes. As she talked, I nervously looked at my feet for just a second. I couldn't help but notice the contrast of my black dress pants and dress socks with the nearly white carpet. Black and white. The pants and socks were part of my pastor ensemble. I was twenty-eight, fresh out of seminary, and very conscious of my young age. To overcome my anxiety, I dressed how I thought a pastor should dress. If I didn't feel old enough to offer pastoral counsel to those more than twice my age, at least I could look like I had that ability. That was my thought process.

Truth is, my neatly pressed shirts and dress socks didn't alleviate my feelings of inadequacy one bit. Situations like these made me uncomfortable. I didn't feel like a pastor. It was almost as if I were a child playing dress-up. Still, I wore them, hoping they would help me fake it until I could make it. So there I was, sitting in the living room of a dying woman, trying to offer some tiny bit of pastoral comfort but instead looking at the colors of certainty—black socks against white carpet.

How was a pastor supposed to respond to that kind of

certainty? I didn't share her optimism. As I listened to her excitement about the faith healer, I worked to hide my skepticism. I grew up in a Dutch Reformed tradition, where the closest thing to a charismatic healing service was the pastoral prayer where people were prayed for by name while the congregants reverently bowed their heads. There was no "Yes, Lord" or "Heal her, Jesus" or even an "Amen" muttered by the people in the pew next to you. Not even a holy "mmm-hmm." The only people making noises during the prayer were the pastor and the kids quietly popping Mentos from their wrappers. The only time we got vocal during a prayer was when we mumbled through the recitation of the Lord's Prayer. I was raised with a deep suspicion of the more charismatic expressions of Christianity.

The more Bernice talked of her hope of healing, the more I found myself burning with frustration about the baseless optimism cultivated in her by some charlatan using God's name to pack a Hilton conference room with people who are desperate for hope. What I knew of faith healing was what I had seen on Christian television stations and paid infomercials—you know, the ones that only come on late at night or early in the morning. The slick-talking, gaudily dressed televangelists—emphatically speaking into the camera, urging some distraught individual to sow a faith seed to guarantee a miracle—stirred a visceral anger in me. I submit that the vilest shows on television are those in which a pastor promises miracles in the name of Jesus for money. Desperate people are easy to take advantage of. They grasp for anything to hold on to, anything that promises a little order in the midst of *tohu wabohu*. I couldn't help but feel protective of Bernice.

Maybe it's because I am a part of a cynical, "seen it all before" generation that instinctively gives such things the side-eye, but no part of me thought this was a good idea. But how do you tell someone who is dying that trying every avenue for a cure might not improve their quality of life? Should you even do it? After all, we take such extreme measures medically—ingesting poison until the very end, hoping against all odds that we'll add a few days to our life, or undergoing surgeries while already frail, employing every measure to be resuscitated for a few more breaths. Why not try a little over-the-top prayer?

Do I correct her? Warn her? Share my concerns? Or do I simply nod my head and feign enthusiasm? Seminary doesn't teach you this in your pastoral counseling class.

"Oh? Tell me more." When in doubt, buy more time.

With rambling, rapid-fire anticipation, Bernice told me about the preacher she had seen on the television and how he had such a wonderful gift of healing and how she couldn't wait to be healed and how you know a friend is a good friend when they're willing to drive you to Cincinnati and expect a miracle on your behalf and, oh, she called the number of the preacher on TV and he sent some tapes after she donated money to his ministry and she would love it if I would take them and listen to them because it might be so helpful to someone just starting out as a pastor.

I told her I admired her conviction. That was the truth.

We made small talk for the rest of my visit. She told me about her work. Bragged about her grandson. Talked about her involvement in the church before I arrived. Before I left, I prayed for Bernice and her trip. I prayed for healing.

She walked me to the door, but before I left, she placed a handful of cassette tapes in my arms.

"Let me know what you think of them," she said, smiling.

I wasn't certain I would listen to the tapes, but I thanked her anyway. As I walked to my car, I concluded that the only thing I was certain of were the questions rolling through my head. Did I fulfill my pastoral responsibility? I never defined myself by clearly sharing what I believed. The words of wisdom I was hoping for never came. I didn't feel like I had provided any comfort or any answers. I came as a man of faith, and I was leaving as someone full of questions.

- Can I accept that God may heal Bernice through the faith healer in Ohio?
- Who am I to say whether God will use this man to heal her?
- Why is Bernice so certain?
- Why am I so skeptical?
- Is my skepticism a sign of a lack of faith?
- What if I don't have enough faith but Bernice does?
- What's the difference between certainty and faith?
- When life gives us more than we can handle, is it okay to doubt?
- Where am I going to find a cassette player?

■ ■ ■

At some point, we all find ourselves with more questions than answers.

Picking up the scraps of life after a broken relationship, you wonder, *What's wrong with me? Why does it seem like everyone else is finding love? Is God ignoring the desire of my heart?*

Sitting with friends who are too young to be terminally ill, you can't help but ask, *Why, God, aren't you healing? Could this happen to me? Did God cause this to happen?*

After a loved one passes away, you sift through their belongings, thinking, *Why does death still exist? Did Jesus really feel this pain when he wept for Lazarus?*

Eventually, we find ourselves wondering, *Do I have enough faith to make it through this?*

Behind this question is a common misunderstanding of a particular kind of Bible verse. These verses imply or state outright that God will take care of us if we serve God, love God, or have enough faith. For example, James 1:6 reads, "When you ask, you must believe and not doubt, because the one who doubts is like a wave of the sea, blown and tossed by the wind." Twisted into a cheap self-help mantra, this verse has pitted faith and doubt against each other as if they were warring barons fighting for control of our minds.

On the surface, it does seem as if that is in fact what the text is doing. James appears to say that if you're going to ask God for something, don't doubt that God will answer your prayer. If you need healing, don't doubt that God will heal you. If you need a job, don't doubt that God will provide one. If your marriage needs mending, don't doubt that God will knit the two of you back together. All you need is faith.

But faith without doubt isn't faith. It's certainty. Faith is faith precisely because it isn't certain. There's mystery and not knowing and contradictions and uncertainty, all mixed with a deep hope in something we cannot see. It's trusting in something we can't verify.

Unfortunately, faith has too often been replaced by certainty. I think Western Christianity unknowingly allowed faith to be hijacked by the Enlightenment—and perhaps it even aided and abetted the process. The Enlightenment prized rational and logical thought. The mind was elevated above all else, and a belief began to spread into the Western consciousness that, with more understanding of the world, we could advance humanity toward flourishing. Science became the trusted vehicle to get us to this destination. The world was dissected, analyzed, and categorized. Truth, if it was truth, had to be verifiable.

Christianity, in large measure, bought into this idea. Believing that the Christian faith was historically accurate, apologists embarked on a journey to prove the validity of Christianity through logic, historical substantiation, and even scientific corroboration. Christianity and the claims of Christ, they argued, were something you could be sure of.

Such thinking led Bernice to a faith healer in Ohio. It drove her to say, "If you believe, God will heal you." Not God might heal you, but God *will* heal you. Belief is the catalyst required to bring about healing. Add enough of it, and the reaction is guaranteed to happen, like hydrogen and oxygen making water in the presence of a burning flame. But without enough of this catalyst, this belief, the reaction, may not take place. Which leads us to ask, "Do I have enough faith?" Or even, "Can I be healed without faith?"

In 2014, a father and a mother in Feltonville—a middle-class suburb on the north side of Philadelphia—were sentenced to seven years in prison after their seven-month-old son died of pneumonia. Herbert and Cathy Schaible's son died after they refused to seek medical treatment because of their faith. Belonging to a nondenominational church that did not believe in medical interventions of any kind, they instead were certain that healing should and would come solely through divine intervention. Tragically, this was the second son they had lost because of the way they practiced their faith. When the police questioned them about the death of Brandon, their seven-month-old son, they were already under probation because of the death of their two-year-old son, Kent.

The church they attended promotes certainty under the guise of faith. Their pastor claimed that wearing seat belts was problematic because "anyplace we are told to do something in case something happens is a breach of faith or denying of faith in God to protect you."[1] This doesn't just apply to seat belts or medicine. It extends even to the use of glasses to correct vision and to the role of lawyers in the courts. The idea is tempting because it's simple: if you have enough faith, God will give you exactly what you need.

When asked why the two children died, the pastor replied, "God's healing power was somehow hindered, because of a spiritual lack."[2]

Would I trust the health of my children to prayers alone? I don't have that kind of faith. On the one hand, I think these parents are crazy. On the other hand, I must admit they have a kind of faith that I don't have. Which, again, makes me wonder, *Do I have enough faith?*

But ultimately that's the wrong question. The question should not be, *Do I have enough faith?* The real question is, *Does God require us to have* that kind *of faith?* And the answer is no.

Prayer is not the only way God works in the world. Medicine exists because God, in his good grace, gave us the ability to develop it. This is part of the cultural mandate that goes back to the creation narrative in Genesis 1 where the man and the woman are told to subdue and rule over creation. Our human efforts are a part of God's progressive creation. In this, God works through prayer *and* through our best human efforts. But the perverted theology that denies material answers to life's problems has seeped into our understanding of what it means to believe. Comparatively, using these material means can look and feel as though I don't have enough faith. And if faith equals certainty, I don't. Those refusing to take their sick children to hospitals have that kind of faith in droves. Not me. I'd be the first in line if any of my kids required medical attention.

Faith is not certainty. Treating faith as certainty leaves us anxious and exhausted in our pursuit to prove we have enough faith. We're forced to shut down a part of our finite humanity—the part that asks questions, has doubts, wonders, and worries. We hide our truest feelings, forced to choose dishonesty over intimacy with God in order to appease him with our cocksure facade. Those who espouse this theology wrap millstones around the necks of hurting people, casting them into the deep waters of inadequacy. More than that, they cast an image of a golden calf, a false god fashioned to quiet their own anxious hearts.

■  ■  ■

Doubt has often been characterized as the dangerous opposite of faith. Doubt, we are told, leads to questions that undermine orthodox truths about God's character. Doubt, we are told, will lead us to abandon Scripture as the only rule for life. Doubt, we are told, will cause us to miss out on the blessings of God that require faith to experience.

Whereas doubt is demonized, faith has become synonymous

with unwavering certainty. Postured like this, certainty becomes an idol. If it's necessary to be absolutely certain, if doubt is an evil to be eradicated, then faith will not save you from the evil you are facing. Certainty will. Being certain that God will keep your kids safe keeps them safe. Being certain that God will provide when you're in need brings provision. Being certain that God will save you ensures your salvation. Being certain that God will heal you—naming and claiming—gets you the healing you've been praying for. Being certain that God will accept you is what convinces God you're good enough. Certainty is an idol dressed up as unshakable faith.

Whatever threatens an idol will be deemed evil. The idol of security will see risk as a threat to avoid. The idol of family will see the other as someone of suspicion. The idol of nationalism sees any identity that challenges one's national identity as a threat. The idol of a simplistic worldview will see education as an evil. And if your idol is certainty, you will perceive doubt as the enemy.

And if certainty is an idol, then we will do everything in our power to protect it. Idols are inherently weak. They exist only because we created them out of our anxiety about the world we face. To endure, they need constant tending. They need us to give them attention. They need us to give them a place in our life. They need us to fear them. Without our veneration, idols crumble. Thus they demand protection. The idol of certainty is no different.

We see evidence of this throughout Christianity. Science is viewed with suspicion because it raises questions about the creation narrative in Genesis, our understanding of what it means to be human, and the miraculous. People who ask questions are labeled as dangerous wolves leading people astray. College and public education are feared because they expose young people to ideas that force them to wrestle with their faith. All of this wrestling and exploring is okay—even good—unless certainty saves you and doubt is a threat.

What if faith isn't ever meant to be defined by certainty? What if mystery and questions and doubts and learning are the fuel of a faith that is able to burn red-hot, even on the coldest, darkest nights?

Some might push back against embracing our doubts, pointing to the first verse of Hebrews 11, which seems to be another call for certainty: "Now faith is confidence in what we hope for and assurance about what we do not see." Certainty, it seems, is central to faith. But is it?

As post-Enlightenment people, we think of certainty as an intellectual assent to an idea based on evidence. We are certain the world is round(ish) because there has been enough empirical evidence to justify our assent to that idea. We're certain that our bodies are made up of millions and millions of cells because, with the help of microscopes, we can see them. We're certain that fire consumes what it burns because we can see the ash it leaves behind. Evidence drives our certainty.

It's tempting to believe the myth of certainty. Rationally, it seems as if certitude about what God is doing or will do can provide hope in the midst of suffering. But any hope it offers is cheap. It rests on superficial claims, prematurely providing "answers" to our deepest questions by trivializing the very real pain we carry. It shortcuts the cross, negating its necessity in providing salvation by selling snake oil guaranteeing a life "free of suffering." But the gospel of Jesus is that in the cross, through the suffering of the cross, life is found. This is a profound mystery. Jesus didn't just go to the cross so we wouldn't have to. Jesus went to the cross and rose three days later so when we find ourselves suffering and crying out to God from our own crosses, we may have hope in ultimate healing through restoration. Real hope, then, isn't some intellectual proposition to believe in. Real hope is found when our faith is hammered out on the anvil of human experience.[3]

Being a follower of Jesus wasn't designed to be based on certainty. Abraham wasn't certain where God would lead him when he left his father's house. Moses wasn't certain he could convince Pharaoh to let the Israelites go. And it's likely Peter wasn't certain what Jesus meant when he was invited to fish for people. Living in the kingdom of God isn't about certainty. It's about relationship. And relationship is founded on trust.

When my wife and I were married, we stood in front of our friends and family and made vows. We were young, deeply in love, and undeniably naive when we pledged to walk with each other in good times and in bad, in health and in sickness, in joy and in sorrow. The future was a mystery. We had no idea what it would hold and no ability to be certain that we would be able to fulfill those promises. We didn't know that one day I would be fired from a ministry position. We didn't know that we would face infertility. We didn't know how each of us would respond to those situations. When we stood, hand in hand, facing each other and making promises about our future, there was no way to know with any certainty what we were promising. Were we certain of our love for one another? We might say we were certain, but there wasn't enough evidence for that. No one outside of us would have had enough evidence to definitively conclude that they could be intellectually certain we would survive life's events.

What we had was trust. We trusted that whatever happened, we would get through it. We trusted that both of us were committed to the relationship. We trusted that together, we would be able to overcome anything.

Faith is not intellectual certainty. It's trust. Faith is, despite all the evidence to the contrary, an abiding expectation in the promises of God. A confidence that he will never leave us or forsake us. That no matter what we see happening around us, the God who created the universe has not abandoned it and has not given up on working good in it. Trust can handle what certainty can't—our doubts and questions.

Faith, then, isn't the absence of doubts and questions, but it's a relationship with such a deep commitment to one another that it can handle the doubts and questions. That's why an evidence-based faith cannot sustain us when the helter-skelter sucks us into its whirlwind. How can you claim to know what God is doing when a young, expectant mother is told that her daughter who'll be born in six weeks has a birth defect that may take her life? How can you be certain that you've got enough faith to convince God you're deserving of healing?

The only thing you can be certain of is that you are laughably unprepared to handle a situation like that. None of us are certain how we will react. None of us are certain we will know what to do. None of us are certain what it will do to our faith in a God who promises good gifts to his children. Nor is certainty going to make those situations easier. Sure, it can promise, like every idol does, to get us through, but it won't. Its lies are cheap. All that certainty will do is separate us from ourselves. Holding on to the idol of certainty with a vise-like grip will cost us our humanity, our emotions, our questions, and our hope.

Faith in Jesus is not based on empirical evidence. It's based on a relationship. Within a relationship, trust is more important than certainty.

■  ■  ■

Honest expression of doubt is often a sign of faith. As Episcopal priest Fleming Rutledge writes, "The very existence of such doubts are themselves a sign of the divine action that elicits the cry, 'Help my unbelief!' (Mark 9:24)."[4]

"Cursed is the one who trusts in man, who draws strength from mere flesh and whose heart turns away from the LORD. That person will be like a bush in the wastelands," writes the prophet Jeremiah.[5] Certainty, in matters of faith, is founded on a trust not of God but a trust of our strength and ability to be certain through intellectually convincing arguments. Suffering will never make sense to our finite minds. We can say, "God has a plan," trying to reassure ourselves that what we've experienced has a purpose. But let's be honest, when a young child dies of cancer or when we see images of a young boy washed onto the shores of some foreign land because his family fled a country torn apart by war, that plan seems problematic. We will never understand why God allows young fathers to get incurable cancer. The fact that one girl is born into a culture where girls are discarded because parents want only sons, and another is born into a culture that celebrates her intelligence and potential, will never seem just. Our explanations for why trial after trial affects one family and not another are empty.

The inability to understand the grand scheme of the universe and make sense of painful and seemingly meaningless events plants the seed of doubt in our minds. Questions will come.

The questions are natural. A few years back, a friend of mine, a pastor, was gathering with members from his church to clean the cemetery next to the church. These are the kinds of small acts of service that endear so many churches to their communities. These were the kinds of projects this pastor, Jaman, was consistently leading his congregation to do. As they gathered at the church prior to starting their work, a woman walked in, asked to see the pastor, and then shot and killed this twenty-nine-year-old husband and father.

During the police investigation, the woman claimed she was connected to a Columbian drug lord who had a connection to the former president George W. Bush. In a wild conspiracy theory, she claimed the former governor of Florida Jeb Bush had killed her grandmother. Her grandmother's murder was somehow, in her mind, connected to the Bushes' involvement in drug and human trafficking. Her reason for killing this young pastor? She believed he was mixed up with the Bushes.

Tell me, what purpose would this death serve? Why would God decide that having their pastor killed in this fashion would be best for this church? Why would God decide that his daughter should be able to read this in the newspapers about her father? Or more pointedly, that it would be better for her to grow up without her father? How in the world would this act move the mentally ill woman who shot him toward redemption? Any sane person would question how this could be a part of God's plan. But too often, we deny our humanity by ignoring our questions. We try to have superhuman resolve as we face uncertainty. We've been taught for too long that doubt and questions are the enemy. That they're a slippery slope. That doubts lead to questions, and questions lead to the possibility that what we have always thought is wrong.

Our beliefs about God and how God interacts with the world are some of the most foundational beliefs a person can hold. Humans are meaning-making machines. We are constantly looking at the world and trying to make sense of what we are exposed to. We connect dots between events so that there is a cause and effect that we can comprehend. Over time, this provides a framework, a mental model of the world. We try to explain that this is how God operates—and this is how we should relate to God. Having a sense of understanding about the world provides security.

But there are times when what we go through falls so far outside of our mental model of the world that pithy statements no longer provide a satisfactory explanation. Our situation falls so far outside of our understanding of who God is or how God relates to the world that we search for new meaning. The search feels like a crisis of faith—and it is.

Job, of the Old Testament, had just this experience. The story goes that Job was a righteous and pious man. He was wealthy and respected, and God clearly cared for him. Job had everything anyone could want. And one day, God allowed it all to be taken from him. His wealth was extinguished, his children killed, and his body ravaged by disease. While Job never cursed God, he did find himself questioning everything he had assumed about how the world worked.

Job understood the world through the framework of divine retribution. Similar to karma, it's the idea that you get what you deserve. God is in his divine courtroom watching the earth below and takes his cues from what he sees happening below. If you remain righteous and follow the commands of God, then God will bless you. Your land will increase, your flocks will grow tenfold, and you'll have many sons (remember, patriarchy). But if you don't, if you ignore God and choose to do whatever you want in the world, then God will punish you. Your wife will be barren. Your flocks will be stolen. Your health will deteriorate.

Admittedly, I share Job's assumption that this is how the world operates. When the needle pierced my wife's abdomen to end the pregnancy we had prayed and hoped for, I shook my fist at God and wondered what we did to deserve this. We're good people. I'm a pastor, for crying out loud. I've given my life to following Jesus and helping others follow Jesus. How could God allow this to happen to us? I know that following Jesus doesn't shelter us from life's storms—I can't tell you the number of times I've preached that sermon. Yet there I was, operating as if that's how the world works. Divine retribution is a hard drug to give up.

The whole book of Job questions the legitimacy of divine retribution. Job adamantly denies he did anything to deserve his agony. His friends counter that he must have done something. He must have angered the gods somehow. He must have some failure he's forgetting about, because that's how the world works. Job demands that God present him with a list of his offenses because, again, he doesn't deserve the punishment he's received.

Job takes all of the questions he has and brings them before God and essentially cries out, "Is this how the world really works? Is this who you are? Are you a cruel God who abandons righteous people to suffering? Is the world fundamentally unjust?" Out of Job's suffering come primal questions about the very foundation of reality.

Very rarely do we allow ourselves to question our most deeply held mental models of the world in the way that Job does. To doubt those beliefs, to question their validity, is, quite literally, world changing. It isn't like having doubts about whether you bought the right house or made the right career move. These questions exist on a whole other plane. Doubting God and your faith is to wonder about the very nature of reality. Changing these beliefs comes at an extreme cost. Most of us aren't willing to pay that cost. Most of us aren't willing to live in the anxiety, to live with the uncertainty, as we allow the Holy Spirit to reshape our understandings. Instead, we grit our teeth and wrestle the doubts into submission. We say things like, "God has a plan," or "Everything happens for a reason," or "Let go and let God" to reassure ourselves and silence our questions.

Silencing our questions is often a form of distrust. It assumes our relationship with God lacks the necessary integrity to sustain the weight of our doubts. And so, with the strength of our flesh, we clench our fists and pretend certainty. Do it for long enough, and you will be like a bush in the wastelands. You and your faith will dry up. The fruit you once bore will shrivel. The green leaves that provided shade to the roots of your faith will wither. The land around you will dry out as you consume every drop of water demanded to support and honor the idol of certainty. Eventually, your faith will die out, and you'll wonder where God went.

Following his indictment of the one who trusts in human strength, Jeremiah goes on, "But blessed is the one who trusts in the LORD, whose confidence is in him. They will be like a tree planted by water that sends out its roots by the stream. It does not fear when heat comes; its leaves are always green."[6] This is the difference between trust and certainty. Recognizing that faith is built on trust allows the questions to exist. It opens us up to a deeper conversation with God. A conversation where we bring all of who we are to all of who God is, and we trust that in that holy, sacred space, what we don't understand will be reconciled to the God who is redeeming all things.

■   ■   ■

A few months after her visit to the faith healer, Bernice died. She was certain, right up until the end, that God was going to heal her. But her certainty did not translate into healing—at least not in the way she would have defined healing.

After her death, I found myself with more questions. Did Bernice lack faith? Should she have gone to another faith healer? Was her true cancer doubt?

Those questions are cruel. They assume we have control over our lives in a way that we don't really have. Faith is reduced to a formula we can manipulate to solve our problems.

After writing about our experience with infertility, I was interviewed by a magazine. Shortly after the article ran, I received an envelope at the church. In the envelope was a note that simply read, "I read your article and thought these would help." Paper-clipped to the note were three tracts: "Faith for Healing, Baptism in the Holy Spirit, Deliverance, Victory over Satan, and Receiving God's Promises"; "The Purpose of Pentecost"; and "Occult, Oppression, and Bondage." Stunned, I glanced back and forth between the note and the tracts. Was this person connecting our infertility to a lack of the Spirit and our practicing of the occult?

I wish I was making this up, but I'm not. At that moment, the church phone rang. I answered, and the woman who sent the note was on the other end of the line. She explained that while she knew I was a pastor, she also knew that people who struggle with infertility, cancer, and mental illness often have dabbled in the occult without knowing it. She stated that if we prayed for the Holy Spirit, we would likely see God remedy our situation. I asked her straight out, "Are you saying that God caused our infertility and we had to choose between ending a pregnancy and my wife's life because we have dabbled in the occult?"

"Well, perhaps you didn't know what you were doing."

Jesus commands us to bless those who persecute us. Don't let anyone tell you it's easy. I'm not sure I blessed her as I vociferously corrected her theology.

Far too often, those who have been crushed by this world are blamed for their misfortune in an effort to find the cause behind their circumstances. And what for? Our own peace of mind? If faith is a formula, then we can solve the problem. If a lack of faith was the problem for Bernice, then if anything like that happened to us, we can avoid her ending by having a better faith. If infertility disrupts your plans, repent of the occult, pray for the Spirit, and get that family growth plan back on track. Every affliction can be solved by fixing your faith when faith is a formula to solve your problems. But in order to hold this view when the formula doesn't result in the desired outcome in a person's life, we must find a problem in that person. We must assign them guilt. Out of our own anxiety we malign the faith of another.

Better to have faith enough to doubt. Faith enough to ask the honest questions. Faith enough to abandon the idols of certainty and control. That kind of faith creates space for compassion toward others. But more than that, faith with room to doubt fosters the authenticity necessary to have our understandings of God transformed.

# CHAPTER 3

# HOW LONG, O LORD?

## *More Anger Than You Can Handle*

From depth of sin, and from a deep despair,
From depth of death, from depth of heart's sorrow,
From this deep cave, of darkness deep repair,

Thee have I called, O Lord, to be my borrow,
Thou in my voice, O Lord, perceive and hear
My heart, my hope, my plaint, my overthrow.
Sir Thomas Wyatt, "Psalm 130"

All around me, scattered on the forest floor, were the drab brown and gray of fallen leaves. There was some snow huddled on clumps of raised field grass that had grown where the trees thinned out, but otherwise the forest floor looked dead.

I'd come to the woods to clear my mind. To think. To be silent. But those leaves with their incessantly rustling static made it impossible. It was March and cold, though there was no snow on the ground as I wandered the small, square lot of mature oaks, maples, and beech trees surrounded by housing developments and a small airport. The nature preserve was a souvenir of the past. I didn't go into the woods to find wilderness—these were not expansive woods where one could get lost without even trying. I simply wanted to get away.

Truth is, I didn't need a vast expanse of wilderness to get lost in. The wilderness had found me.

■  ■  ■

My wilderness was circumstance. It had been less than a week since my wife and I rode the emotional roller coaster of finding out she was pregnant, being told something was wrong, and confirming something was wrong. It had been less than a week since we'd been told that the child would not survive and that if we did not end the pregnancy, my wife's life would be at risk. It had been less than a week since I held her hand in the emergency room and the needle pierced her side.

We cried for days after that morning in the emergency room. Still feeling pain, Sarah rarely left the bedroom. While she was lying in bed, I would sit next to her, but I didn't know how to do much more than sit. I had never felt that helpless.

Infertility has a way of reminding us how much of life is beyond our control. Science doesn't guarantee success. For all our medical advances, doctors remain mystified as to how the miracle of life begins. They know the necessary ingredients. They can swirl them together in a test tube. But to actually make life begin? We've yet to figure out that catalyst. Which is probably the way it's supposed to be, but for me, in that moment, running my hands through my wife's hair as we wept, the illusion of the ability to arrange our lives according to our dreams felt like building sand castles in the rain.

This is what wilderness feels like. It feels like being in the desert, with the taunting voice of the Liar as your only companion. It feels like wandering for forty years without any certainty of your final destination. It feels like seeing your most dearly held hopes and dreams collapsed into rubble as you are carted off to some distant land. It feels like everything is burning and God has abandoned you. It feels like Job's lament: "I cry out to you, God, but you do not answer; I stand up, but you merely look at me."[1]

My wilderness was confusion.

My wilderness was anger.

My wilderness was unfulfilled desires.

My wilderness was wondering where in this emotional hell God could possibly be.

It seemed as if God was only looking at us, not acting, not fixing our situation.

■ ■ ■

Sarah's parents had come into town to help with our son. Needing to process everything, I went into the woods.

The path led me along the creek, where the forest transitions to field, and through an old marsh. The more I walked, the more I needed to get somewhere. Somewhere different. Away from here. Away from the path.

In the last week, my life had gone off the path. This wasn't where God was supposed to lead us.

"In all your ways submit to him, and he will make your paths straight."[2]

"Watch the path of your feet and all your ways will be established."[3]

"In the path of righteousness is life, and in its pathway there is no death."[4]

How was this the straight path? How was ending our long, prayed-for pregnancy our established path? There was death here, so were we even on God's path? No, it was time to get off this path.

I charged through the brush, through the slick mud that sat atop the frozen ground. I turned my back to the briars, pushing past the tiny needles that were trying to ensnare me. My pace matched my heart's fury.

I was emotionally raw, angry, and confused, and I needed space to clear my head and say what was on my mind.

My body said what my voice couldn't. My anger, my confusion, and my desire for space were all driving my body forward. And my direction matched the clarity of my thought: *I'm going everywhere and nowhere.* I had no destination in mind, but I was going to get there.

My breathing got heavy. I slowed my walk and noticed my body heaving steam from the mouth, like a volcano threatening eruption.

I distracted myself by finding trees that had been rubbed by deer. In the fall, male deer viciously rub their antlers against small, young trees—on red maples and small willows. Beside marking territory, it's a deer's effort to remove the dying, velvety flesh from the hardening bone that will become its antlers. As the tree's bark wears away, the white, soft core of the tree is exposed to the world like a wound.

The diversion worked for a while. But suddenly, I was returned to the reality of my own wound. The tears felt hot on the chilled skin of my face. They came unexpectedly. The force of my emotions surprised me. With white-hot anger, I screamed to God from my wilderness, "You tell us that you knit us together in our mother's womb! But you failed! How come this child didn't even get into the womb? That's on you!"

I don't think I have ever talked to God with that kind of clarity, that kind of candor.

And immediately I felt ashamed.

■　■　■

Growing up in the Reformed tradition taught me to believe deeply in the sovereignty of God. I was taught to believe that nothing comes to be that God has not let pass through his fingers. So when life falls apart, we dress our emotions in our Sunday best and act as though the mess is not in fact a mess. We masquerade as though everything is exactly as it should be.

In the scheme of eternity, of course, we believe it is. But in our most primal flesh-and-blood moments, it feels anything but neat and ordered. Nothing has shaken my faith—not in Jesus, the cross, or the resurrection, but in my chosen theological system— like this ordeal. Years later, I am still reeling. Still processing. Still trying to figure out how God's goodness and sovereignty inhabit situations in which we are so clearly pressed under the weight of a world that is not as it should be.

In such moments, it is hard to make sense of why God allows events like these. We have to say God allows them if we believe God is sovereign. That isn't to say that God acts as a divine puppeteer. God isn't manipulating ISIS to heinously murder twenty-one Christians, causing a police officer to shoot an innocent man out of fear, playing the economic market so a company cuts jobs, or speeding up cell reproduction in a tumor.

While hyper-Calvinistic representations of Reformed theology may carry the idea of God's sovereignty to this extreme, they grossly misrepresent most Reformed—and indeed biblical— thought. God "causes" the tragic events in the world to happen insofar as he caused humans to have free will. Once he gave humans free will, God no longer exists as the only active agent in the world. You and I have agency.

In the beginning, God tasked Adam with naming the animals. Later, Adam was told to work the ground and take care of it. God didn't dictate what he should name the animals. Ever since, humans have been involved in the work of cultivating the world. God invited us to continue God's creation project. God didn't deliver a meticulous list of instructions about how to take care of the world. God entrusted us with an ability to choose. We have been empowered to act in freedom in the world.

Yet God is sovereign. And sometimes it seems as if he chooses not to act. Sometimes it seems as if he only looks at us.

That is why we must say that God allowed these events to happen. Even if you believe that God has limited his power and knowledge about the future or has chosen to step back from the world to create space for humans to act in freedom, you have to say that God, in his choice to limit himself, is allowing evil to occur. We cannot rationalize away the seeming connection between a transcendent, all-powerful God and the presence of evil in the world. If God is all-powerful, there isn't any way to get around the fact that he has the ability to stop evil and suffering, and yet he chooses not to.

Which means there are times when the only one you can blame is God.

Before you think I just committed a heresy, consider for a moment the psalms.

Why do you hold back your hand, your right hand?
  Take it from the folds of your garment and
    destroy them!

                                                    Psalm 74:11


Awake, Lord! Why do you sleep?
  Rouse yourself! Do not reject us forever.

                                                    Psalm 44:23


My God, my God, why have you forsaken me?
  Why are you so far from saving me,
    so far from my cries of anguish?

                                                    Psalm 22:1


Again and again, the psalmists seem to hold God responsible for the hardships they're subjected to. When the helter-skelter engulfs us, the psalms provide a model of authentic faith. Forty percent of the psalms are cries of lament. With brutal force, the psalmists voice the deepest pain, the most honest questions, the most candid engagement of God as sovereign in the midst of suffering. Deep calls out to deep. Through lament, we bleed from the cuts of this world's jagged edges.

Lament reveals the overwhelming nature of our emotions and our hunger for hope, but also our understanding of and our trust in God. Those of us who grew up reading Scripture have been told that God knows the number of hairs on our head.[5] He cares for the sparrows of the air.[6] He dresses the flowers of the field.[7] God is intimately familiar with us and our needs—which means that, in his omniscience, God is acutely aware of the darkness we walk in.

It is exactly because we believe that God is sovereign that we can lament. God has promised to redeem and restore the world. He has promised to defeat evil. He has promised to dry every tear from every eye. So when our news feeds fill up with horrific events, and when our lives feel plagued with tragedy, it's okay to say it doesn't seem like any of those promises have been, or are being, fulfilled. Suffering surrounds us; death is all too present; too many tears are being shed. God's promises, it seems, have not yet been fulfilled. That's on God.

So we lament. And in our lament, we blame God for allowing evil and suffering to still exist. We cry out. We scream because he has, for some unknown reason, allowed the world to swirl in a violent vortex around us.

After all, if God wanted to, evil could be extinguished forever. So we are left with three options: (1) God is not sovereign and is unable to change the events and circumstances of this world; (2) God is sovereign but chooses not to exert his power on our behalf, and we, mere objects of his will, are unable to utter any legitimate grievance about our situation; or (3) God is sovereign but chooses not to exert his power on our behalf, and we hold God responsible for that apparent choice.

Now when we say we "blame God," we should be clear about what we mean. We don't mean we have determined God to be guilty of not fulfilling his covenant promises. We aren't declaring that God isn't good or trustworthy. If we decided that God was not good, then we would no longer expect any good from him. There would be nothing to lament. Nothing to complain about.

We blame God because we still trust God to be good. Our blame is the deep, guttural cry of our pain in the form of our most honest, raw questions. If the Lord is good and has promised to deliver us from evil, then why are so many still anguishing under evil? If God is the healer, why hasn't he healed? If God is with us, why does he seem so far away?

These questions do not show a lack of faith or trust. Just the opposite. They show an incredible amount of trust as we refuse to abandon the promises that God has spoken. In our pain and confusion, we do not blame God as the source of our pain, but we blame God and protest the reality that evil exists in the world that God is holding in his governing hands.

Lament is also not the same as gross bellyaching about one's situation. Again, the psalms serve as a wonderful model for us. As theologian J. Todd Billings writes, "The psalms of lament are not like the grumbling of the Israelites in the wilderness, who displayed a lack of faith in God's promises. Because of their faith in God's sovereignty, the psalmists have high expectations of God; because they take God's promises seriously, they lament and protest when it seems that God is not keeping his promises."[8]

Our natural response to suffering is to ask, "Why?"—"Why did this happen to me? Why did God allow this to happen? Why does this pain have a place in God's plan?" Lament does not guarantee that our questions will be answered on our timelines. Instead, lament is a tenacious witness to the hope we cannot see, to the resurrection we have not attained, and against the power of sin in the world.

■   ■   ■

Three years after I shook my fists at the sky in the woods, I co-led a retreat for pastors in Ontario, Canada, that included a session on being authentic with God through a life of reflection. I'd been working with these pastors for about three years, so there was a high level of trust and authenticity among us. While the content we had was good, my coleader, Marijke, and I began feeling as though we had blocked out too much time for this session. We also sensed from the participants that we needed to switch up our approach. So after a break, we spontaneously decided to have an unrehearsed conversation in front of the whole group. This wasn't an ordinary conversation. Marijke was going to coach me.

"Can you tell me a bit about your spiritual practices right now?" she began.

I took a deep breath. Even though I'm a pastor, I don't really like talking about my spiritual life. Blame it on my Dutch heritage—reserved, taciturn, private. That would be the easy thing to do. But honestly, I often feel shame about my discomfort. Quiet reflection and slowing the pace of my life enough to pay attention to God don't come naturally to me. They are practices that I am still learning. As a pastor, I feel as though I should be practicing at a varsity level, but I'm still playing kindergarten "bunch ball"—where young kids crowd around the soccer ball and try to all kick it at the same time rather than spreading out across the whole field—instead of soccer.

"Since we're talking about authenticity, I'm going to be authentic," I joked. "Engaging the spiritual practices are hard for me. Especially lately."

"Why do you say *lately*?"

"Some practices come easier than others. Reading and studying—these have always come easy for me, and I continue to make space for them in my life. But others are harder. Prayer. Silence. They just aren't a part of my rhythm right now. It's not that I don't want them to be or that I don't think they're important. There's something else there that—and let me say I wasn't planning on sharing all of this in front of everyone today—there's something there blocking me. It feels as though I'm resisting entering into something that feels that intimate."

"When was the last time you felt like you had really been praying?"

That question opened my eyes to what I couldn't, or wouldn't, see.

"Around the time Sarah had the ectopic pregnancy."

I could feel the emotions rising and rushing over me. It had been three years since that needle pierced her side. We should have moved on. I should have gotten over the anger and the frustration. But I hadn't. Time created the space for me to pretend that the absence of the pain meant there was no reason to be present to my grief and anger. I'd tricked myself into believing that suffering is only marked by the acute presence of pain.

The presence of suffering is difficult to discern. Some of us have grown accustomed to its company and, in ways that astound others, disregard its impact on us. Some of us know we are suffering, but we're also acutely aware that others are suffering too. With a tendency to compare ourselves to others, we determine that their suffering is greater than ours, and thus we downplay how much we are hurting.

To be clear, suffering is more than pain—physical, emotional, mental. Suffering is a reality whenever our ability to flourish is stolen from us. Being barred from voting in one's country and having a voice that is represented in government is a kind of suffering because flourishing is limited. Throughout history, people have supported kings even as that same king imposed taxes limiting their ability to make a better life for themselves.

A single mom who tirelessly works to meet her children's needs—and does meet them!—but does not have time or space to care for herself isn't flourishing. Kids whose parents are uninterested and uninvolved are missing out on the love and nurturing they need and deserve. Suffering includes the experience of pain but is not limited to it.

Far too often, though, we only admit we are suffering when the presence of pain is undeniable to us and to those around us. Then, as good, self-reliant Americans, we feel the need to "pull ourselves up" and "get on with it," denying the emotional and spiritual agony that lingers long after the afflicting affair is over. Remove the obvious calamity—a tornado destroying a town, the consequence of our own poor choices, or a relationship that came to an end—and we expect suffering to come to an end.

"Why has prayer been hard for you since then?" Marijke pressed.

"Because I'm still angry with God," I blurted out. This wasn't scripted. I wasn't planning on saying this as a pastor to a group of pastors. I would never have planned this moment, because it made me look bad. But a hidden geyser had been tapped, and now everything was coming out.

"I suppose I should be overwhelmed with gratitude because everyone is healthy and I have a great family." I paused, trying to process what I was feeling.

There is an unspoken pressure to dance, smile, and thank God for his faithfulness. That's what good Christians do, isn't it? We pray our angsty prayers, longing for God to meet us in our pain, to bring resolution to the conflict of our story, to miraculously swoop in and light up the darkness. And after our prayers have been answered in some form, the fear and frustration and anger that fueled our fist-shaking shouts to the Almighty will combust into delight. Because joy comes in the morning. The rainbow spans the sky after the storm. The child cries after the labor pains.

At least that's how the story is supposed to go, isn't it?

Except that at the time I was leading this retreat, we'd been waiting five years for another child through birth or adoption. For five years, my wife and I had prayed, hoped, and dreamed for our family to grow. It broke my heart whenever my son asked when his baby brother or sister was going to come live with us. God heard that, right? He saw us, right? Yet we felt no reassurance that our prayers would be answered. We just wondered whether we should move on from this hope. We'd suffered infertility and an ectopic pregnancy. Now we waited.

I started talking again.

"Waiting is its own kind of suffering. There's a quiet helplessness as you sit on your hopes, asking if they're going to be relegated to the realm of pleasant daydreams. Five years of wondering if the God we call Father, the God who loves families, the God who encourages us to care for children, was listening to us. So honestly, it just doesn't feel like praying did any good."

I got quiet. I could feel my cheeks had flushed in shame. It felt as though I had violated some unspoken Christian rule about not being mad at God. Perhaps this is why honesty in churches and small groups is so uncommon. And not the polite honesty that admits we don't read our Bible enough, but the real honesty about our doubts, fears, and angers. There is a shame in expressing views contrary to the illusion of happiness cultivated by shiny, Instagram-ready churches. No one wants to be the dissident.

But I could also sense that the air in the room had shifted.

Looking around, I didn't see judgment in people's eyes. I saw compassion. Understanding. I didn't think I'd said anything profound. I had simply been honest. But the authenticity of my lament created a sacred space.

We began talking about bringing all of who we are to all of who God is, right here in a generic hotel meeting room. Except we were now standing on holy ground in front of a burning bush.

Lament transports us to holy ground. But we have to be willing to stand before the fire. And more than that, we need to be willing to come close enough to feel the heat of the flames and trust that we will not be consumed.

■  ■  ■

Four years into my pastoral ministry, I presided over the funeral of a woman in her early forties who had lost a three-year battle with cancer. As I stood in the pulpit and looked at her family and friends, I was overcome by the thought that this wasn't right: *I shouldn't be doing this funeral—not for someone this young. Young children should not lose their mother. A father should not have to grieve his wife and comfort his children. Cancer should not exist. Death should not be.*

Something primal in us longs for a world untouched by grief, tears, death, and injustice. Deep within our bones, a voice tells us this isn't how the world is supposed to be. Perhaps *voice* is too strong a word. Often it's quieter than that. Maybe it's a whisper. An echo reverberating through our souls. An ache without origin or location. A dream we know we've had but can't fully recall.

God did not create the world with death as a part of his good design. When God placed the sun and the moon and the stars, the trees and the fish and the land animals in the garden, he did not create a place for death. It was never part of the intended design. Death came as a curse—after everything else had been declared "very good."

That whisper, that echo in our souls, could be the enduring ripple of those words. That creation was *very good*. This is not. We feel it.

This is why I love Easter. Easter expresses a future hope in the resurrection of all things. "Where, O death, is now thy sting?" we sing, dressed in our Easter pastels. As our voices rise, our hope is kindled in the world that is; we exist between the world that was and the world that will be. Death was not present in the garden and will not be present in the new creation. One day, "God's dwelling place [will be] now among the people, and he will dwell with them. They will be his people, and God himself will be with them and be their God. He will wipe every tear from their eyes. There will be no more death or mourning or crying or pain, for the old order of things has passed away."[9] This is our hope. But it isn't realized yet.

Many use the Easter story as a way to escape reality. We have churches in our town that have their Easter celebrations on Good Friday. I know they do this as a practical solution for accommodating the larger-than-average Sunday crowds, but there is a theology implicit within this liturgy: Death can be avoided. Good Friday is unnecessary.

Cultural practices like this feed what I call "a religion of triumph." This religion masquerades as authentic faith. Gathered in the pews of First American Do-It-Yourself Church, we sing songs designed to make us feel joy even though we feel like weeping. Testimonies only move in one direction: "I was drunk in a ditch and now I'm drunk on Jesus." Sermons are peppered with stories of how applying the pastor's cleverly worded points will make your life better. This is the dominant religion of America—the religion of triumph.

So we find ourselves with a faith that glosses over pain. The myth that Christians always have a song of joy to sing is perpetuated. The complexity of this world is exchanged for a framed, cross-stitched cliché atop a meadow of flowers. The whole human experience—both the raw and the profane—do not need to be lived. They can be sidestepped because Easter is here.

Using platitudes to endure hardship is a form of denial. Pain cannot be soothed unless it is felt. What's torn cannot be mended if the rips and tears aren't acknowledged. Resurrection cannot happen if one does not or will not die. Christianity does not avoid death. It goes through death and then rises to new life.

Religion is often used to avoid suffering. But that's not Christianity. Theologian Douglas John Hall argued that "the basic distinction between religion and faith is the propensity of religions to avoid, precisely, suffering: to have light without darkness, vision without trust and risk, hope without ongoing dialogue with despair—in short, Easter without Good Friday."[10] The incarnation of Jesus assures his followers that we will never truly escape the human experience. God embraced the human experience fully, experiencing joy, suffering, work, play, and even temptation, just as we do. Thus, wholeness is found when we enter fully into our humanity too—the tragic, painful, and unfortunate.

Good Friday reminds us that Jesus, the Son of God, experienced what we experience. On the one hand, that's comforting. But on the other hand, it is a disconcerting thought. Jesus suffered. Jesus was humiliated, was wounded, and bled. We don't really want a God who shares in our weakness. We'd prefer the strongman who is able to hold a storm at bay. But our God rushes right into it and—as he shows us what it means to be human—calls us to follow him. We will be betrayed by those we love most. Our bodies will be a canvas of scars. We will cry the cry of dereliction, "My God, my God, why have you forsaken me?"[11]

Others lose sight of the hope the Easter story gives to the suffering. Unable to see past their situations, they give up believing that anything good can come from the rubble of their circumstances. What they can see, hear, touch, smell, and taste is all there is. The tangible blots out the possibility that there's more to reality than what our senses can comprehend.

Whatever our reasons for wanting to avoid suffering, let's be honest: we will all have our Good Friday.

Those who truly want something new to come from the ashes of life must be willing to live in the tension of the "already but not yet." Easter people must also be Good Friday people.

Most of us are some combination of both of these people. We are caught in the in-between in a Holy Saturday world. Even as Easter people, we live between confusion and clarity. Between hope and despair. Grateful we aren't who we were, but guilty we aren't who we should be. We're trapped between the ache for the unblemished garden and the future hope of every tear being wiped from our eyes by the gentle hand of God. We live between death and resurrection.

Hope feels dangerous in a Holy Saturday world. Like leaning too far over a cliff without a rail to hold on to. Often our hope feels unfounded. What we see and experience doesn't give us the confidence to lean out over the chasm. So we back away from the edge, and in doing so, we back away from hope.

Lament is our lifeline, providing the tension to give us the confidence to lean out in hope. Counterintuitively, certainty doesn't provide that security. Yes, we would prefer our suffering to be explained. We'd like to know why it happened or what good thing will rise up from the ashes. Perhaps if we possessed that information, we'd persevere with more courage.

Explanations are the mythical gold pot at the end of the rainbow. They're the things that push us to cling to the false hope that logic and reason will save us. But even if we did know why God allowed suffering in our lives, it wouldn't negate the grief and pain.

What makes lament superior to certainty is that it clings to nothing other than the hope. It requires the Divine to intervene on our behalf. But to properly lament, we have to be awake and fully present to two realities: what is and what will be. When what is and what will be have little in common, we lament. We incarnate our words with the full brunt of our emotions. We bring all of who we are to all of who God is. Like the models of faith found in Moses, Abraham, and David, we hold God accountable to his promises. Like Jacob, who wrestled with God, we say, "I will not let you go unless you bless me."[12]

Lament requires transparency that can be as terrifying as our sufferings. But I've come to believe that faithful followers of Jesus must be forthcoming about difficulty and pain. We may not always want to be honest about the world. There is a temptation among Christians to talk about faith as the solution to life's problems. To paint a picture of life with Jesus where only sunshine exists. Only music in major keys will be played; dancing rhythms are a must. Nothing will break. Nothing will hurt. Nothing will die.

But I also want everyone to know Jesus. In order to tell people about Jesus, I need to be honest with them about the world that is. Because where they meet Jesus is in this world—the real world. The one with scraped knees and broken bones. The one with lies and betrayal. The one where we feel more like fish caught in the net of chance than sons and daughters of a present and attentive God. If I want people to meet Jesus, I have to let them live in this world, because that's where Jesus is. He isn't at the edge of some fantasy world. He isn't even on the margins of this real world. When Jesus came into the world, he put himself right into the middle of the whole damnable world, right into the middle of the worst of it. If we want to find Jesus, then we must walk right into the middle of it as well.

Lament requires that we stand fully present to the flames before us. And the hope of our lament is that Jesus will be standing there with us.

■　■　■

My voice echoed back to me off the trees. I heard the woods again. The wind blowing through leafless trees sounds like a child learning to whistle while holding his lips too far apart. I heard a squirrel running in the leaves. The woods are rarely, if ever, silent. Listen carefully enough, and the cacophony of sounds will overwhelm you. Like the woods, I'm rarely silent. But now I was silent.

I spoke my peace in the wilderness and then stood listening to the silence in me. In that moment, it didn't all begin to make sense. Years later, I still don't know why God did not guide that child into the womb and then into our home. God didn't speak into the quiet gentleness of that early morning. No explanation has been offered.

Perhaps this truth is our only remedy: God is less interested in our understanding the "why" behind our situations than he is in having an authentic, honest, open relationship with us.

It's important, then, to remember the story we find ourselves in. In this story, God takes the formlessness and emptiness, the *tohu wabohu*, of life and makes something beautiful. This transformation began with the act of creation, when God formed the formless, brought light to the darkness, and controlled the seemingly uncontrollable. In the beginning, the Spirit of God hovered over the raging waters of chaos and tamed them.

As we remember this story, we remind ourselves that we, too, are caught up in a story of reformation and resurrection. God hovers over the wild chaos brought about by death and destruction and corruption, and he pledges that it will not consume us. God has promised not to abandon us to the grave, but out of the ashes of our grief and pain and suffering will come new life and beauty and grace and glory.

I still don't know why everything has happened the way that it has. I don't know why we had to end the pregnancy. I don't have even a clue as to what the purpose behind these events may be. But I do believe that God was, and is, hovering over us. Better yet, God is with us.

We may hope to skate through life without experiencing financial worries, illness, betrayal, or death, but we know these are unavoidable. Intellectually, we understand that, in a world that is broken, it's not a matter of *if* we will suffer; rather, it's a question of when. Life's jagged edges will cut us.

Unfortunately, the church, the very institution that claims to understand and explain God's movements in and through this world, often pressures us to muster the pretense of unshakable confidence. That God is going to heal us. That God will fix our situation. That God will right the wrongs that have been done to us, in all the ways we envision.

Instead of giving the sufferer space to lament, our grief is shut down by the glib reminder that "if we just have enough faith, it'll all work out." We are called to mourn with those who mourn, but too often those who mourn are prodded to get on with their grief so they can experience the joy of the Lord. We aren't comfortable with grief work. It produces anxiety. It necessitates questions. To be present with those who have questions is to be present with their questions. And that makes us nervous. Rather than sit in that place of tension, we ask those who are mourning to move themselves somewhere happier so we can be more comfortable.

Underneath this practice is the belief that human suffering can be overcome by proper technique: *Suffering isn't reality; it's the absence of the proper outlook*; or *Change your perspective, and you'll see suffering doesn't really exist*; or *Adopt a technical understanding of God's promises, and you'll be able to claim the best God has for you.* These mind-sets are pervasive in America's self-help, rugged-individualism, "pull yourself up by your bootstraps" culture, but they also have a deep hold in the American church. Combined with the American prosperity gospel—where you reap what you sow, where your faith allows you to "name it and claim it"—our imaginations about how God relates to pain and suffering repackage blatantly cheap theology into more pious and theologically palatable sentiments.

The theologian Paul Tillich said that "it is impossible for a finite being to stand naked anxiety for more than a flash of time."[13] Shielding ourselves from suffering and pain is a coping mechanism. The world is more than we can handle. In our anxiety, we resort to technique. If implemented correctly, an orderly, step-by-step process will render tragedy obsolete—or so we believe. Thus, we cover over our anxiety with plastic smiles, physical and emotional distance from tragedy, a cause-and-effect faith, and manicured lawns.

But a technical faith will not sustain us in the midst of life's darkest moments. Most of us don't have an eternally optimistic outlook on life. That isn't to say we are irredeemable pessimists, but most of us are realists. Facing terminal cancer, we aren't easily convinced that the miracle will be ours. Walking through a failed relationship, we do not believe that instilling a proper perspective will produce the reconciliation of all things. Staring at unpaid bills, it's hard to believe that our daily bread will be there tomorrow. In fact, when life gives us more than we can handle, the most central claims of our faith are the hardest to believe.

Inside of us a voice says, *This isn't the way it is supposed to be.* That is the beginning of our lament.

# CHAPTER 4

# THE DEEPEST DESIRE
## *More Desire Than You Can Handle*

"What do you want? What do you want?" he repeated to himself.

"What do I want? To live and not to suffer," he answered.

Leo Tolstoy, *The Death of Ivan Ilych*

Eric was feeling despair. Looking death in the eye, he saw not only his future but also the futures of those whom he loved the most. It was a future that did not include him. As he talked, the room closed in on this painful, holy moment.

The living room walls were paneled with wood and the carpet was brown. It could have given the room a dirty and claustrophobic feel. Instead, the warm lighting, the portraits and pictures on the wall, and the big windows made the room feel wide open and inviting. To my left sat Eric and his wife, Kelly. Marv and Carol, Eric's parents and members of my church, sat to my right. Eric's body bore the markers of many chemotherapy patients—sunken cheeks; thin, smoky pale skin; and a bandana covering his hairless head.

With the final stages of lung cancer becoming a reality, I was meeting with Eric and his family to offer whatever pastoral solace I could. We talked briefly of the treatments tried and the options that were no longer available. Hospice was the only remaining choice. But we didn't talk of these things long.

Faced with the finality of life focuses our remaining time on what matters most. Everything unimportant gets stripped away. The nearness of death can be like putting blinders on a horse. There is so much in life—so much to look at, so much to do— that we take our eyes off the most wonderful things. Everything screams for our attention. Happy to oblige our hedonistic sense, we spend our lives whipping our heads around in a vain effort to take it all in. But death changes how we see. The bright lights, shiny trinkets, and tantalizing distractions are blocked out by the blinder of limited time, and we only see what's most important. It's all we want. We're no longer interested in seeing everything there is. We desire only to see what's most beautiful.

Eric began to talk of his daughter and son. Tears began streaming down his face. "Dying is one thing," he said, "but I can't accept that I won't get to be at my kids' biggest events. I won't see my kids graduate from school. I won't teach them how to drive." And then Eric broke down in sobs. "On my daughter's wedding day, I won't get to walk her down the aisle."

We spend much of our lives chasing after the comforts of the world. After the success that will give us meaning, the possessions that mark our place. We trick ourselves into believing that these things ultimately matter. Our valuable time and energy is taken up by getting the house fixed up, saving for a new car, making sure our kids are on the best travel sports teams, and fretting over how the landscaping looks. When you're looking at death, a grand reversal of life's priorities takes place. Whereas before you'd tell your son you couldn't go fishing because the lawn needed mowing, now you'll let the lawn go wild for one more trip to the pond. You spent so much time chasing money, but now you'd do anything for another hour to sit with your daughter. Once upon a time, you'd step back to reflect on the promises of God and focus your soul on the hope of the resurrection only after you cleaned out the attic. But now, who cares about the attic? If death ever gave us a gift, it's the clarity to see what really matters.

Our conversation turned to faith. Eric admitted that religion and faith weren't always the priorities they should have been, but he was clear: he had accepted Jesus as his Savior. The longer I serve as a pastor, the more important these small statements of faith have become to me. Cynicism isn't hard. It'd be easy to write off these simple statements of faith as a fear-induced grasp at hope. But maybe that's exactly what faith is.

A central refrain in the Bible is that we should "not be afraid." God seems to understand the predicament of being human—fear is always there. It's so central to being human that I can't help but wonder if the low level of fear we call anxiety wasn't present in the Garden of Eden.[1] Ask yourself, *Why was the temptation to be like God so compelling to Eve?* Christians have long been taught that it was pride, the desire to become like God. And surely there is truth to this. But why would Eve want to be like God? Is it because the anxiety and fear of not knowing what tomorrow would bring subtly gnawed at her just before she fell asleep at night? Did the dependence on another being for everything produce just a tinge of anxiety, just a bit of fear, in her? In Adam too?

Believing that faith ought to be birthed free from fear or death-bed conversions is a kind of pipe dream. We've got anxiety and fear about something. Maybe it's dying. Perhaps we fear a life without meaning and purpose. Or it could be that we feel out of control and need to believe that someone is in control. If we were to dig deep enough, I think we'd find that we've all got something we're grasping for. I'm coming to believe that's okay. As Douglas John Hall wrote, "Hope, when it is real, presupposes an ongoing dialog with despair."[2]

As I listened to Eric, I couldn't tell what was causing him more pain: the thought of dying, or the awareness that the desire to be present in his kids' lives would go unfulfilled.

■  ■  ■

When life is more than we can handle—when cancer is found, a job is lost, a relationship disintegrates, and the unexpected stuff hits the fan—and you hit your knees in prayer, what is it you want? What is the deep desire of your heart?

On the surface, the answer may be an obvious one. We want what's broken to be fixed. We want God to hear our prayer, wave his divine magic wand, and heal the illness. We want our prayer interrupted by the ringing of the phone with an employer offering a job on the other end. If we are honest, this is what we want.

But is that what we really desire? Absolutely. In the moment, that is what our heart longs for, and it may even be the most immediate need we're facing. All that is true. And yet it's also true that whatever we are praying for isn't our deepest desire. Usually, and we may not be completely aware of this, there's a desire behind our spoken desire.

I have a weird quirk—whenever I travel, I want to get a souvenir of some sort. Part of this impulse is that I like to spend money. Again, an odd quirk that has been with me since childhood. My mom likes to tell a story of me as a child, three or four years old. I couldn't read, but I wanted to put money in the newspaper machine just to get a newspaper. I'm 100 percent Dutch—a people known for their frugality—but based on my affinity for spending money, you'd never know.

One summer, my family took a two-week trip to tour Yellowstone and Glacier National Parks. At Yellowstone, we stopped at one of the many souvenir shops in the park. I wandered the store for what seemed like an hour—it was probably less; there's no way my parents would allow me to shop for that long. I was looking for the perfect trinket to buy. The more I looked, the more distraught I became. When my dad demanded that I hurry up and make a decision, I begrudgingly bought a coin purse—one of those round, rubber things with a slit on one side that when you pinched it, it opened up. Yeah, that's what I, a ten-year-old, bought. It's still a joke in my family. But funnier to me is the fact that my dad still has it. Why? Because he's a better Dutchman than me.

Did I want the change purse? No. It was never about the change purse. I had a desire to remember the trip. A piece of rubber kitsch was a tangible way to keep the memory alive.

The true desires of our heart are often hidden from our consciousness. We think we want the new car. So we research, read reports, compare makes and models. We go out and test-drive, visit different dealers, talk with the bank, and pore over our finances. For weeks, maybe even months, we dream of the new car. The day comes and the purchase is made, and then we drive off the lot. While we may enjoy the new car, it doesn't satisfy us. There's something else that we begin to desire. Maybe a new TV, a boat, whatever. On the surface, it seems that our desire is for the thing, whatever it might be. But dig a little deeper, and we may find that the true desire wasn't material at all; the true desire was the pursuit of something else.

Or take a gambler. Why do they throw down their money hand after hand? To win seems like the obvious answer. But if you could wave a magic wand that made it so a gambler never lost a hand, how long do you think they would find the blackjack table enjoyable? Eventually, they'd get bored. The true desire of their heart wasn't to win; it was the struggle to win. The anticipation that the next hand would be the one to break the house. Take away the struggle and uncertainty, and the gambler loses interest.

Jeremiah tells us that the "heart is deceitful above all things."[3] Our truest desires, motivations, and hopes are often disguised by the trappings of less permanent things. In our creation as image bearers, we are predisposed to long for the things that last—beauty, truth, goodness, hope, faith, love. The pursuit of all that is eternal is etched into our hearts, and in the absence of those things, we find the gaping hole of eternity aching to be filled. But the heart is indiscriminate in that it will substitute the thing it most desires for something less. Its deceit is that it will fool us into chasing what religion calls "idols"—money, sex, security, family, adventure, success, fame, and the like—to fill that gap of eternity.

Even the prayers we pray at our most honest moments often fail to express what we really want. We pray that God will heal. But more than that, we want to know that God is listening. After all, until Jesus returns, another sickness will come. Lazarus, the friend whom Jesus brought back from the dead, eventually died again. Better to know that God is listening than simply be healed.

Prayers that God will free us from addiction may be good and right, but perhaps a deeper prayer sits under those prayers: *God, be enough.* Prayers for provision may be natural and justified, but perhaps driving those prayers is a deeper prayer: *God, see me.*

When Jesus taught us to pray longingly for God's kingdom to come, for God's will to be done, on earth as it is in heaven, he expressed our ultimate desire. We pray for healing, but we want no more sickness, just as it is in heaven. We pray for reconciliation in a relationship, but we want the shalom of God's kingdom. We pray for relief from financial difficulties, but we want assurance of our daily bread, as it will be at the final banquet table. Ultimately, we desire these things.

But do we deserve what we desire?

■ ■ ■

There were twenty or so of us in the room. Some sat on sofas and chairs that lined the walls; others were on the floor. Plastic Nalgene water bottles, Moleskine journals, and leather-bound Bibles gave this away as a gathering of college students. We were the unusual students who didn't migrate south to a beach for spring break. Instead, we were making our way to New York City for a mission trip.

We were ready to do God's work, praying for blessing, asking God to do what only God can do, pleading with him to make a difference in the world through us. There was a naive urgency in our intentions. We were going to sweep into the Big Apple and bring the kingdom of God with us.

I grew up singing, "This little light of mine, I'm going to let it shine." Mine, as if I possessed it. Mine, as if you didn't have what I did. Mine, as if I were some generous philanthropist because I'm willing to share. I was taught to be so pious that I couldn't see my self-righteous air of superiority.

Marty, the adult sponsor on the trip, was one of those men

who enjoyed a supernatural ability to examine your mind and heart despite your best efforts to keep your secrets hidden. He was tall and slender, his hair cut a quarter-inch longer than a buzz, with a scar from a cleft palate; he was completely unassuming from a physical standpoint. But when we prayed, he became a force. He was a presence that could not be ignored. It is said that the Lord looks not at our outside appearances but at the heart, and if you could see Marty's, you would see the heart of a warrior.

There was an ebb and flow to the prayer. People would pray back-to-back for minutes on end, followed by long periods of silence. During one of those times of silence, Marty spoke. Quietly. Firmly.

"There is someone here who has been filling their life with something that is not satisfying them. There's a picture in my mind of an empty cup, and this person keeps putting something in it, hoping it will fill the cup, but it doesn't. The harder they try, the more shame they feel. The more empty they are."

Looking back, I can see how this statement could be like the vague, ominous pronouncement of a cheap fortune teller, carefully worded to apply to anyone's life. But in that moment, I had no chance to process it that way. Sitting on the floor with my head bowed, my eyes flashed open. The primal portion of my brain screamed, *Danger!* Adrenaline pumped through my veins. My heart raced, my muscles tensed, my vision narrowed in on my shoes.

I became a deer that sensed a threat, ready to bolt into the woods. I didn't want anyone to know that Marty was talking about me. I knew what my sin was, and I was ashamed.

In college, temptations are many. Porn was mine. I had fallen into the abyss and found myself wanting. Thinking it was something I could do in the dark, something that would be hidden from the eyes of others, I forgot that the dark is not a comforting blanket. The lie is that we can hide in the dark. We cannot. We can only lose ourselves in its vast emptiness. This is what it means to be lost, and I was lost.

I sat very still. *No sudden movements*, I thought. *Don't give yourself away.*

I felt like the kids in *Jurassic Park* when the Tyrannosaurus rex peered into the car window. Don't move and he won't see you.

Slowly, I lifted my head, almost casually, as if I just need to shift positions. My eyes opened, and the first thing I saw was Marty looking right at me.

His eyes locked with mine. He pointed his finger at my chest, nodded his head slowly, and then put his head down.

I looked around to see if anyone had seen what just transpired. I expected to find people staring at me, mouths hanging open with questions. Apparently, everyone else was more devout than I was; they all had their eyes closed. No one saw that I had been seen. But I felt like the woman at the well who had just been told that she had five husbands. Who was this man who knew my secrets?

I realize now that was the wrong question. It wasn't this man. No, the question was, Who is this God who saw me and wanted to occupy my heart?

My mind didn't make its way back to the prayers being offered. Instead, I wondered if we could ignore what had just happened. Would Marty say anything if I said nothing? Would I be able to carry on as if the moment had never taken place? Could I tell Marty that he was wrong? That he had the wrong person? Or perhaps I could just confess my sins to God, ask for forgiveness, believe that my sins would be carried away from me as far as the east is from the west, and this would all be over. That's how it works, right? Just a quick prayer of confession? Isn't a silent acknowledgment of my infraction all that is necessary for grace to overwhelm me?

I hate to put anything past God. That said, I've rarely seen a sick person get better without first acknowledging that they are sick. Confession is the admission of sickness. It's also more than that. Episcopal priest and author Robert Farrar Capon writes, "Confession is not the first step on the road to recovery; it is the last step in the displaying of a corpse."[4] The apostle Paul says that we, in our transgressions and sins, are dead.[5] The dead cannot bring about their own rehabilitation. We like to think we can, which is why resurrection is such a difficult concept. It's otherworldly, because in this world we accept the notion that any change in our lives must be done by us. Resurrection, on the other hand, is done *to* us. But only once we are dead.

Therein lies the scandal. Private confessions to God are attractive precisely because I don't have to admit to the larger world that I am dead. Powerless against the darkness within me. Unable to bring order to my own chaos. I need the God of death and resurrection to come into my death. That's what Good Friday and Easter are about. Jesus enters our death so that, with him, we may be given new life. If we want to experience this resurrection, then we must admit that we are dead.

We finished praying and said our amens, and then everyone stood. I knew what had to happen. Mustering up every ounce of courage I had, I walked up to Marty.

"Can I talk to you?"

"Absolutely," he said gently. "I'd love to."

I put my corpse on display in front of him. Told him of my shame and the void in my soul and what I was trying to fill it with. Later that week, I told the entire mission team about my darkness. And I received words of affirmation from so many members of the group, but mostly—and most surprisingly— from the women. I was filled up by the forgiveness they offered, the encouragement they spoke, the prayers they prayed.

Something unique happens when life is more than we can handle. We dredge experiences up off the ocean floor of our past and question the meaning we gave to them. Fifteen years later, trying to wrap my mind around ending a pregnancy, I found myself thinking about this moment in life and wondering if I was being punished for that sin. What I thought I knew about grace and forgiveness no longer anchored me. The theology I studied failed to hold up against the waves. The doctrine of justification—which is the forgiveness of sins through Jesus' death on the cross—is built on grace. Yet there was no grace beyond my salvation. Grace removed my sin as far as the east is from the west. Grace meant that God would not remember my sins as I entered into glory.

But it seemed grace was having nothing to do with my life when it was more than I could handle. My life was still the accumulation of my sins. Sin was still working death in my life. And because of my sin, the ectopic pregnancy, the infertility, and the confusion my wife and I were experiencing is what I deserved.

Suffering can turn our hypotheses about God into proven facts in our minds. We may wonder if God is an impersonal karmic force that ensures balance in the universe, and the isolation we experience proves that God is uninterested in us. God could be an accountant tediously keeping a ledger of all our rights and wrongs and simply doling out the wages one has earned. So when cancer invades our body, it is obvious that God has determined through careful arithmetic that we ought to be punished. Whatever portrait of God we held in our minds is confirmed through suffering.

When we think of God as an impersonal force or an accountant of our sins, God is the opposition to our desires. It is God *or* our desires. Or they are the carrot that God dangles in front of us to keep us in line. Our dreams for a family, our longing to have meaningful work that is satisfying and uses our talents, the want we have for close friendships, the wish to not have to worry about our finances every month—all these things are spoken about in whispers, lest God hear and take them away. They are God's leverage over us. If we want them too much, he will take them away as punishment—maybe even as punishment for wanting them too much. So we stamp out the yearning and convince ourselves that we are *not* worthy of the desires of our hearts.

Every one of us has some deep-down, dark secret sin that would anger a ledger-keeping God. Some of our sins have been dragged into the light, while others still lurk in the shadows. Either way, we've all got reasons to believe we don't deserve to have our dreams fulfilled.

But God isn't a ledger keeper. And we don't always get what we deserve.

■ ■ ■

That question haunts me. *What do I deserve?*

The Christianity I grew up with taught, definitively, that we, incorrigible sinners that we all are, deserve death. Our sin offends God. It is a prideful rebellion against the Creator. "The wages of sin is death,"[6] Paul wrote, and for most of my life, I've been told that is exactly what I deserve. No matter how good I try to be, no matter how many mission projects I take on, how many little old ladies I help across the street, or how much money I give away, my good deeds are not enough to warrant anything other than death.

I've wondered what sin Paul is talking about when he uses the word *sin*. Is he talking about that incurable disease, the genetic flaw of sorts that distorts the image of God? Or is it my sinful behavior? Is God placing my sinful acts on a scale opposite my good deeds and watching with a careful eye to determine which side tips?

I suppose it doesn't matter. The worker deserves his wages, and we have all too often put ourselves in the employment of our sin.

The predominant understanding of sin and salvation depicts the dynamics as transactional. In the divine economy, we exchange our sin for God's salvation. The currency that enables this transaction is the blood of Jesus.

The apostle Paul tells us that "while we were still sinners, Christ died for us."[7] The gospels tell us story after story of how Jesus dined with sinners, dignified prostitutes, and touched the unclean. The gospel of Jesus is more than news about a transaction.

Salvation is even more audacious than just having our sins forgiven. As much as our sin affronts an all-holy God, sin doesn't separate us from God. If "neither death nor life . . . nor anything else in all creation, will be able to separate us from the love of God," then *nothing* can separate us.[8] Not our worst deeds. Not our best intentions. Not my mistakes. Not your most shame-filled moments. Truly, nothing can separate us from the love of God. Our sin doesn't happen outside of the saving grace of Jesus, but within its omnipresence. To use the metaphor of light and dark, all the deeds of darkness are done in the light of Jesus. Jesus truly is God with us. No matter where we are, no matter what we're doing, no matter what we're going through—God is with us.

But this doesn't always jibe with our understanding of reality. We cannot fathom a world where we do not get what we deserve. Our world only works by finding worth in what we do or do not do. Did you do your job well? Then you deserve a raise. Did you study hard, seeking to learn the content beyond being able to regurgitate it on a test? Then you deserve a good grade. Were you kind to the right people? Then you deserve kindness. Did you play the role of a faithful spouse? Then you deserve a storybook marriage.

Getting what we deserve makes absolute sense in a world that often doesn't make sense. This is why we are drawn to karma-like thinking or the principle of "reaping what you sow." It provides a clear map to navigate the world. If you work hard, you will be rewarded with everything you want. With that proven map, we know what we must do in life. Work. Earn. Secure. Prove ourselves worthy.

Under this paradigm, life is reduced to a project of our pride. We focus on what we have done in an effort to make sure we get exactly what we deserve. We give ourselves to assertiveness and vanity, grumbling and caviling when we're denied what we think we are owed.

Or we use the principle to justify ourselves and look down on others. "The poor are poor because they've failed to work hard," we say. In other words, they deserve their lot in life.

■ ■ ■

The day was gray. Clouds were hanging low over the city, and the wind blew up and down the streets. The group of college students I was with on the mission trip were on the corner of a park in New York City, serving food to homeless folks who lived in the area. I struck up a conversation with a young man who looked to be in his late twenties. He wore a long black peacoat, a tan stocking hat, and gloves. From the stubble of his beard and the freckles on his face, I gathered he had red hair.

I was struck by how thin he was. Not emaciated, but thin. His eyes weren't sunken, but they were dim. As we talked, he curled his hands around a cup and blew the steam off the surface of the coffee.

"Can I ask how you ended up on the streets?" I tentatively inquired.

"Sure. I'm an artist. I struggled like most do and just couldn't make it."

"I'm sorry to hear that. Do you have family or anything?"

His eyes dropped. I had inadvertently touched something tender.

"I don't talk to them anymore." He paused. I could tell he was weighing whether he wanted to share with this college-aged do-gooder about his situation. He did.

"I'm gay. When they found out, they disowned me. A while back, I found out I have HIV. Between that and not making enough with my art, I ended up out here." He looked around to indicate the streets.

We chatted some more, but my mind was reeling. What did I have for this man? What did I think of this man? He was the man I'd heard sermons about. The one who was a character on television. He wasn't real to me before this moment. But now that he was standing right next to me, what was I to do?

He said he needed to go. He took off his glove and extended his hand to me.

What he said earlier rang through my head. "I have HIV." I looked at his hand. His fingernails were a bit long with dirt under them. His hands weren't rough. Dirty, yes, but soft. They trembled. Perhaps from the cold, or perhaps from the vulnerability of inviting someone to meet his desire to be treated like he deserved—as a human being. I had just confessed my sexual sin to a group of acquaintances and strangers on the trip with me and was forgiven and accepted like I was family. This gay man's hand trembled in the cold because his family couldn't accept him.

I took off my glove and shook his hand.

■　■　■

Our culture teaches that the man I met on the street deserved his circumstances. The American Dream is predicated on the belief that hard work and good choices will lead to success. Achievement is based on performance. This is America's karma. If you don't succeed, it's because you made a mistake. Thus, his choices directly led to his plight.

Despite our best efforts, we are always influenced by the surrounding culture. We'd like to think that our spiritual lives are like a pristine, secluded mountain spring whose water is free of contaminants. But we swim in the stream of our culture. Our minds and souls are affected by all that's upstream from us. For this reason, we can't help but have our imaginations shaped by America's karma.

It can be too easy to live with a "grace for me, karma for them" approach to those who have been beaten down by life in ways different from us. Even the most ardent Christians have allowed some version of karma to influence their understanding of the world. Revolt all you want against such an idea, but even the Scriptures seem to imply a soft karmic mechanism driving the world forward. "A man reaps what he sows," Paul writes.[9] In Deuteronomy, God promises that if you obey his commands, he will send blessing through agricultural success.[10] Worship other gods, and the skies will hold back their rain and the ground will fail to produce a crop. You get what you deserve.

Could there be more of a karmic sentiment? Put the seed of goodness into the ground and blessing will spring forth, providing a harvest of good fortune. If you sow wickedness, don't be surprised if judgment comes your way. Obey God and be rewarded; disobey and be punished.

Asking "What have I done to deserve this?" reveals the insidious pervasiveness of our belief in karma. Bad things don't just happen to good people. We, like Job's friends, try to find the catalyst to our pain. There must be some sin, some unconfessed transgression, some act that angered God so that he turned his back on us. Maybe we didn't pray enough. Maybe it's because we haven't been to church in six months. Maybe we've been a little stingy with our money. The possibilities for upsetting the Almighty are endless. But whatever the case, we are convinced there must be something, because—despite labeling karma as a pagan heresy—logic necessitates some cause to our pain.

Karma is not compatible with the Christian notions of grace. Karma and grace are antithetical. Yet because we live in a world that is merit-based and market-driven, we cannot escape simplistic, cause-and-effect thinking. In fact, there's something soothing about it. Something that removes ambiguity about our worth in relationship to others. Cause and effect, getting what we deserve, allows us to think better of ourselves and quickly pass judgment on others without pricking our consciences.

This is where the idea of what we deserve runs amok. Far too many preachers have spoken with the wrath of hell on their lips about the deserved death of the totally depraved scumbags who fill their pews. "The wages of sin is death" is breathed over the congregation as a fiery threat. And there's truth in that statement, to be sure. But we must come to see that this isn't a tit-for-tat, cause-and-effect, pay-for-what-you-get proposition. If sin is inseparable from the human experience, if "all have sinned and fall short of the glory of God,"[11] then death is our current state of being. What I mean by that is this: we cannot save ourselves any more than a corpse can walk. We cannot rectify all the wrongs of the world any more than a corpse can bandage up their wounds. With death as our state of being, there is no longer the transaction of our sin for death. Once we remove this idea from our minds of a necessary transaction in the spiritual realm, we can separate ourselves from the question, "What do we deserve?" once and for all. We don't deserve death. We *are* dead.

Coming to realize this is the first step in discovering what it means to truly live. When Paul writes to the Philippians that we are to "do everything without grumbling or arguing, so that you may become blameless and pure, 'children of God without fault in a warped and crooked generation,'"[12] he is imploring us to lay aside this language of jockeying to make sure we get what we deserve out of life. Grumbling when we get less than we think is ours, complaining when people less deserving in our eyes get more than they should—this only leads to death. As German theologian Karl Barth wrote, "The Word of Life is death to the poisonous germ of *all* self-glorification."[13]

Embracing this death is the first step to "shine like stars in the sky."[14] For it is how we reflect the life of the One who did not seek his own life and glory but made himself nothing and gave himself up for us.[15]

Once we give up our pride project, we begin to see that all this talk about what we deserve misses the point. Jesus followers aren't distinguished from others simply because they made a better choice about what to believe. It's isn't that we have some secret knowledge about the world. It isn't that we are morally superior. Rather, Jesus followers shine brightly because they have given up the desire to be superior to their fellow human beings and have chosen to treat everyone as worth-filled image bearers. All this is a fancy way of saying that those who follow Jesus treat people the way that image bearers deserve to be treated. Our cue in how to treat others is found in how God has moved toward us.

Thankfully, God has never dealt with us in terms of what we deserve. For that we should rejoice. Rather, God has acted toward humanity as if we have worth. "For God so loved the world that he gave his one and only Son, that whoever believes in him shall not perish but have eternal life."[16] This most well-known of Bible verses communicates the incredible worth ascribed to us by God. God's self-sacrificing act proclaims unequivocally to the ends of the universe that those who bear his image have indescribable worth and value. Not just those who have deserved it, but *all* those who bear his image

We are left, then, to "work out"—practice, try on, or keep learning about—our salvation "with fear and trembling."[17] Simply put, we ought to be humble. We deserve death, but at the same time we are deemed worth saving by the One who sent his only Son to die for us so that all who believe will have eternal life.

And the big dirty secret is that what we deserve does not change what we are worth in the eyes of God. Like any father or mother who loves their children, God sees us as worthy of all his love and affection. Working out our salvation is the continual work of living out of that value. With fear and trembling, we begin to think of ourselves as valuable enough to pursue. With humility, we treat others as valuable enough to die for. All of our relationships and dealings with people begin from a place of recognition of just whom we're dealing with—someone whom Jesus deems worthy.

Can you imagine a world where everyone treated each other with that much dignity?

Can you imagine if you were secure in the truth that you are that worthy?

And as if that isn't good enough, God takes it even further. In Christ, our deepest desires will be met, and we are given far more than we deserve.

**DOUBTING OUR DOUBTS**

*More Faith Than You
Can Handle*

CHAPTER 5

Why, after wounding
This heart, have You not healed it
And why, after stealing it,
Have You thus abandoned it,
And not carried away the stolen prey?

John of the Cross, *A Spiritual Canticle*

Every church has one person known as the resident saint. Our church has Monty. Extroverted to the extreme, Monty is one for whom there are no strangers; there are only friends she hasn't yet met. No one is unwelcome at her house. Every Fourth of July, her backyard is filled with people enjoying her pool, her food, her house, and her hospitality. Her ability to make people feel comfortable in her presence knows no limits.

But that's the second thing you notice about her. The first thing you notice is her faith. Talking about Jesus is never far from Monty's lips. Her greatest joy is sharing the good news about Jesus—especially if she gets to tell someone about Jesus for the first time. I've been on airplanes with her and seen her legitimately disappointed because the person next to her is already a Christian.

Monty's faith is not the thing of clichés. It's simple but tried.

Straightforward but tested. Prior to my arrival as the pastor of the church, Monty's husband had been tragically killed in a car accident. Almost a year later to the date, her oldest daughter was killed in another car accident. Just a few years after these unthinkable tragedies, Monty is still faithfully serving her church, dreaming about a room filled with people worshiping Jesus.

I once asked Monty if her trials had ever led her to question whether God was good. She looked at me like I had just asked her if she had ever tasted purple. "No," she said. Her response caught me off guard. It didn't seem real. That's the kind of thing people say to pastors because they believe it's what pastors want to hear. So I pressed her.

What came out was more nuanced. It isn't that she doesn't think the loss of her husband and daughter are tragic. She hasn't forgotten; she still thinks of them and what happened. Often. The wounds still hurt, and she's quite honest about the ache that expectedly and unexpectedly overwhelms her heart. And yet even with an unwavering faith, she doesn't cover over her faith with plastic optimism. Yes, despite everything Monty went through, her faith in God's goodness never wavered. There is a tension between her grief and her hope that gives her faith an uncommon vitality. She grieves, but not without hope.

If you asked me to create a faith with the tensile strength to withstand breaking when stretched as far as Monty's, I'd be clueless where to start. And I don't think I'm alone. Most of us don't know how to make faith. But our lack of knowledge doesn't keep us from attempting to manufacture something that looks like it. Lord knows that pastors and spiritual leaders labor tirelessly to produce faith in their congregants and followers. There are Bible studies and sermon series galore, all promising the right recipe to bake up the kind of faith that will withstand life's storms by mixing the best Bible verses with just enough of the right theology, stirred with a generous amount of logical arguments. Paul says faith is a gift, but that seems too easy and doesn't fit with our American "pull yourself up by your bootstraps" ideology. We prefer a faith we can control. We prefer a faith we can produce. Parker Palmer points out that our imaginations are defined by manufacturing: "We make time, make friends, make meaning, make money, make a living, make love."[1] If we can make everything else, why can't we make faith? All we need is to get the recipe right, and we'll bake up a faith able to withstand tragedy.

But our best efforts to create a bombproof faith are neutralized by our efforts to tame the chaotic world we live in. We're a people discipled by science. Our understanding of the world is defined by our five senses. But faith doesn't materialize from what you can hear, see, taste, touch, and smell. Going back to chapter 2, that's *certainty*. We're certain of what we can discern with our senses. We don't have to take it on faith that flowers smell good, sunshine is bright, or puppies are cuddly.

We're also taught to be anxious about tomorrow. In anxiety, not in faith, we buy insurance for every possible scenario that life presents, the goal being the mitigation of pain by controlling the future. But what you can control doesn't require faith; it simply requires diligence and good prudence.

Perhaps the apostle Paul was right; perhaps faith is a gift. We can't make it. We can't force it to appear. We can't recite an incantation on behalf of another person that will grant them faith. All we can do is receive it—or when the *tohu wabohu* swirls and we need something to anchor us, grab hold of it.

Or perhaps since every gift must be received, I could say I've struggled to willingly receive the gift of faith. My ego, my self-reliance, my distraction, my anger, all get in the way. I am my biggest obstacle. Whatever the case, my faith doesn't come easy like Monty's. Monty has the kind of faith held up in church as the gold standard. And there are people who possess that kind of faith. Not all of us do. Those of us who don't have an unflinching, unwavering faith are often left wondering if ours is second-rate, inadequate, or even faulty. Sermons and stories about "the gift of faith" leave us questioning if we ever got the gift. Anxiously we speculate if we're a part of "the chosen."

I believe the gift of faith is offered to everyone. And yet life has taught me that not all of us will grab on to faith to anchor us in the helter-skelter. It's there, like a life ring thrown to a drowning man, but you've got to reach for it.

Reflecting on my life, it's safe to say faith hasn't been a gift I possess. My faith has often been chased down and wrestled with. Like Jacob wrestling with the angel, I've had to pin down my faith and demand something of it.[2]

■ ■ ■

More than two years had passed since the night in the emergency room when we ended the pregnancy. For the most part, life continued its march forward without fanfare. Our son entered preschool. Sarah continued to work as a dance instructor. I navigated what it meant to pastor a church and write with regularity. Life fell into a rhythm, and it was good.

And yet, under the surface, a desire to have another child in our family still existed. It's hard to describe, but there was a missing component to our family. Like summer without ice cream, steak without a Cabernet, or marriage without sex—life was good, but incomplete.

Sarah and I attempted to get pregnant again, but our efforts weren't as concerted or as sustained. While apprehension was the unspoken factor of our decision, there was true excitement as we began to consider growing our family by other means. Before we were married we had talked about adoption, so we revisited those conversations with new earnestness. We prayed and discussed, considered and dreamed, about the possibility. More and more, our hearts warmed to the idea.

We began interviewing adoption agencies to learn about each agency's practices, how they found birth mothers, the services and resources they provided birth mothers—both prebirth and postbirth—and whether we felt we could trust the social workers involved. After many conversations with a multitude of adoption agencies, we began to fill out the necessary paperwork required to become active—a term meaning we were approved to adopt according to the agency. While the mountain of paperwork required was overwhelming, the excitement about a child coming into our home powered us through the tedious work of data collection. Applications, bank statements, questionnaires, home studies, physicals—we were like squirrels gathering acorns for winter, scrambling to get every piece of paper required.

And then we were listed as active, ready at any moment to accept a child into our family. All we had to do was wait.

And wait.

Church, preschool, dance classes.

Wait.

Swim lessons, visits to the gym, a vacation.

Wait.

Soccer games, meetings, date nights.

Wait.

Home studies—the report the social worker writes up confirming you are fit to be adoptive parents—are only good for one year. At the one-year mark, we updated our home study.

Kindergarten, publish a book, recitals.

Wait.

When we started the adoption process, we were told the average wait time was eighteen months. Our decision to go with a smaller, local adoption agency all but guaranteed we would be subjected to the fullness of that period—or longer.

Life continued but was also put on hold. We had planted this stake in the ground, and we could only move so far from it. Time went by, but it felt like life didn't move. Like a dog on a leash in the backyard, we had some freedom and things we could tend to, but we could only go so far. We were tethered to this stake, unable to forget it was there. Conversations of the future could only go so far before the leash went taut and we were pulled back to our stake.

But we tried to live normally. We bought a new house and moved across town to be closer to the church. The move required our home study to be amended, but since we were closing in on the two-year mark, we decided to do a full update. We showed the social worker around our new home, pointed out the covers on the electrical outlets, told her where we would put baby gates to fence off the stairs, and showed her the nursery. After the tour, we sat in the living room to chat before she left.

Curious, we asked how the agency was doing matching babies to families.

"You know, it's been weird," she said. "We haven't matched a baby with an adoptive family in more than a year."

I looked at Sarah. She looked at me. I could see it in her eyes. I could feel it in my chest. Disappointment.

I think the social worker caught the glance we gave each other. "Actually, that's one thing I wanted to talk with you about today. You might want to consider working with an additional agency. We can keep you active with us, but our list of families waiting to adopt is growing, and yet the number of birth moms we're working with isn't. Things could change at any moment, but it's potentially going to be a longer wait than you anticipated."

As she left, we thanked her for her honesty. It's hard to describe what we felt as we closed the door behind her. Resignation began to wash over us. Were we closing the door on adoption? Was what we'd been doing the past two years trying to force something outside of God's will to happen? What were we doing wrong? Were we not praying enough? Why wasn't God answering this prayer? Was our desire to grow our family selfish? Should we begin to accept the idea that we would be a family of three?

The questions loomed large and weighed heavy. Especially on my wife.

■ ■ ■

Those who suffer face a decision: trust that God will not let the present chaos destroy them or sink into despair that God has abandoned them and the future is unredeemed. This choice is an inevitable and necessary aspect of faith. We don't get to know with any certainty what the future holds. As finite creatures, we're bound to the limitations of time. We get the present, even if only for a fleeting moment. Our lives are marked by an enduring posture of readiness for something we hope for but cannot see.

We're tasked with the mundane work of waiting and letting "the past become the present and the present give way to the future."[3] Our life is not one that is, but one that is becoming. Seeds to plants. Grapes to wine. Wheat to bread. Death to life. The present is always giving way to the future.

Woven into the fabric of creation is the mystery of resurrection. For something new to occur in the future, the present must, quite literally, die. We cannot hold on to the present any more than we can hold on to the world itself. To trust in resurrection is to trust in what we cannot see. As finite creatures, this is not a comfort. We crave security that is tangible. We do not want to trust our future to what we cannot see. We trust in full bank accounts and growing 401(k)s. We trust in guns and a strong military. We trust in locked doors and alarm systems. Anxiety causes us to desire something more permanent—or at least something more tangible—that we can trust to protect us as the winds of chaos swirl around us.

Contrast this with faith. Faith exposes us to the harsh elements of wind and rain. Faith demands that we feel the full force of this world. If our faith is never exposed to difficulty, if it only exists in the protection of our suburban lives, then it's simply a mental exercise. We look at a person like Monty and we want her faith, but we don't want to be cast into the deep waters that compel us to grab hold of that faith.

When we're introduced to Job in the Old Testament, we are told he was a man who "was blameless and upright," who "feared God and shunned evil."[4] From the get-go, Job is thought of as a man of faith. Job's reverence for God was so great that God encouraged Satan to consider Job as the model human. I've got a million theological questions as to why God would bring one of his beloved to the attention of Satan, but that's not for us to unpack here. Instead, note Satan's response in Job 1:9–11:

> "Does Job fear God for nothing? . . . Have you not put a hedge around him and his household and everything he has? You have blessed the work of his hands, so that his flocks and herds are spread throughout the land. But now stretch out your hand and strike everything he has, and he will surely curse you to your face."

Think back to chapter 2 where we noted that Job had a karmic view of the world. Blessings were a sign that you were in God's good graces. The way you got into God's good graces was by being a good religious person, which Job was. So when Job had all his blessings taken from him, he could not understand what God was doing. Job was good, and yet God seemed to be punishing him. The world was not functioning the way that it was supposed to. God was not living up to his end of the bargain as Job understood it. Job's untested belief was that faith brought blessings.

According to the text, Satan has this same understanding of the relationship between God and people, only it's reversed. Satan believes that Job loves God and has faith because God has blessed him and protects him. Satan hypothesizes that the moment you take all of Job's blessings away, Job will curse God to his face.

Satan is the ultimate cynic. In Satan's mind, people aren't faithful. They only use faith to get what they want. People aren't romantic. Romance is only a way to satisfy primal lusts in a socially acceptable manner. Leadership is never about the greater good, but about power and self-serving interests. Compassion is about manipulation. The cynic cannot see goodness but instead finds the dark motivation behind the best human virtues. So when Satan sees Job, he doesn't see a man who fears God and shuns evil; he sees a man who is concerned about his wealth and who enjoys the hedge of protection God provides.

In Job's culture and in ours, prosperity is married with faith. Prosperity gospels and their kin are abundant in America. Despite the best efforts of theologians and pastors, the idea that God will give us our desires, will heal us if we have enough faith, and will bless the righteous is all too common. Popularly called the prosperity gospel, it is a kind of *theodicy*—an explanation for the problem of evil. In fact, some would argue it's the dominant American faith because it aligns so nicely with the American Dream.[5] Work hard and you will be blessed. Be good enough, have enough faith, and you'll be blessed. The prosperity gospel and the American Dream are perfect bedfellows.

The book of Job reveals the fallacy of the prosperity gospel. From the beginning, both Satan and Job are trying to determine the true nature of faith: Is a faith that loves God for God's sake possible? Or are humans destined to love God because of what God can do for us? To answer these questions, blessings and faith must be pulled apart like two entangled fighters. Job's blessings must be pulled away from him in order to see if his faith is tied up with them. If this didn't happen, we wouldn't know how deep his faith runs or how strong it is, even if it is sincere. As philosopher Eleonore Stump writes, "A person with great but untested moral, spiritual, or psychological excellence has strength; but, without the exercise produced by testing, endurance is undeveloped or at least unclear."[6]

Faith is refined in hardship. It's easy to believe something when life is going well. It's not hard to believe God is sovereign when your family is getting along or your bank accounts are full or your health is stable. When everything is going well, the idea that God is in control of the world is easy to believe. But I wonder if that's faith. Faith isn't really necessary in those moments. Certainly gratitude is real when everything is idyllic—but faith? Faith is unnecessary.

Faith, the Bible says, is hope in things that are unseen.[7]

Faith is born in the darkness and difficulty.

I'm certain this isn't something you should offer as a kind of comforting explanation to those beaten down by life. But it is a gift to know what you have. It is a gift to realize how strong you are. It is a gift to know you can survive the storm when the winds blow. I just wish there was another way to receive this gift without having to endure the chaos.

It just hasn't been my experience.

■  ■  ■

A couple of weeks after the social worker had been at our house, we went to my parents for Thanksgiving. It was a relaxing time, but I could tell Sarah was unsettled. She was distant. Unusually withdrawn. Throughout the day, I would check in with her. She'd tell me she was all right, but then admitted she felt off. Anxious even. I could see something in her eyes.

We didn't know it, but this was the beginning of a new storm forming over us. The helter-skelter was beginning to swirl.

When meteorologists talk about weather, they often talk about high and low pressure systems. High pressure systems exert downward and outward pressure on the earth. This pushes rain and clouds away from their center. High pressure systems are associated with clear, sunny weather. Conversely, low pressure systems are like vacuums, sucking up everything around them—wind, warm air, condensation—and coalescing into a counterclockwise funnel in the sky. Think of the shape of a hurricane, the quintessential low pressure system.

Suffering is often rightly referred to as a storm. It's not just the chaos we feel that causes despair; it's the fact that everything in life gets sucked into its vortex. We suffer when there is a vacancy caused by unrealized desires, loss of something or someone, or the removal of health. Life becomes defined by what's missing. The vacuum of order, peace, comfort, understanding, and control unmoors our anchor, blowing us about on the wind-driven waves. Everything around us gets sucked into this void; energy, thoughts, and time all get caught in the circling maelstrom of our pain. And just like a storm, the energy brought about by the low pressure has to be released. The sky has to break open, and the rains have to fall. The *tohu wabohu* must rage.

The anxiety Sarah felt at my parents' house grew. Sleep became difficult. She would sit at the table during meals and bounce her leg, something she had never done before. The nauseous pit that settles in the stomach as you stand before a crowd to speak became a constant feeling for her. Her mind raced. She obsessed about every worst-case scenario regarding our family, adoption, her parenting, and even our marriage.

I could see it in her face. Her confidence was replaced by worry and helplessness. Her shoulders seemed pulled down and forward by the taut rope connecting her to that stake we drove in the ground. Weight slipped from her body as the anxiety nullified her appetite. I watched my wife wither and turn brown like a leaf in October.

I once again was rendered helpless. I could hear her anxiety in her breathing at night. Short, staccato breaths just short of hyperventilating. At night I'd lie next to her and wrap my arms tightly around her to control the shaking. I'd place my hand on her chest to try to calm her through loving pressure. I'd tell her to breathe with me as I exaggerated a slow, rhythmic breathing for her to mimic. I'd pray over her. So many prayers. I'd plead with God on her behalf for a moment of respite. An hour of uninterrupted sleep.

Nothing worked.

There were times when she would start to fall asleep. As I held her, I could feel her muscles start to relax. First, the tension released out of her shoulders, down her arms, through her hips. Her breathing would deepen and slow. Just about the moment I'd begin to thank God, she'd violently jerk awake. Her legs would spasm. Sometimes she'd sit up. The internet told me these were called "hypnic jerks." This sounds like they were simply involuntary movements brought about by the gentle suggestion of hypnosis, but this was not the case. The internet would do well to label these conclusions more accurately as "torture." I'm not being dramatic. Repeatedly waking people up when they're on the verge of sleep is a form of torture. Only for Sarah, it wasn't some sadistic individual toying with her. It was her own mind and body revolting against her.

Sarah and I knew she needed to sleep, but she couldn't shut her mind off enough to doze off. She became anxious about trying to sleep. Every one of us has experienced the frustration of needing to sleep and not being able to. We stare at the clock by our bedside and say, "If I fall asleep now, I'll still get six hours"; "If I fall asleep now, I'll still get five hours." What Sarah experienced made that game look tame.

It was a vicious cycle I named "the spiral." If we could just get Sarah to sleep, we might be able to lower the amount of anxiety she was feeling. But she wanted to sleep so badly that she kept herself up thinking about sleeping—which, of course, increased her anxiety. We began staying up all night. We called the doctor and got a prescription for sleeping medication. It worked one night. Only one night. And then nothing worked. We tried everything—melatonin, Ambien, trazadone, chamomile tea, massages, essential oils, alcohol. Nothing worked. At one point, Sarah was awake, having had little sleep to speak of for seventy-two hours, yet full of drugs designed to tranquilize her. It was hell.

I can't describe what the ordeal was like for Sarah—that's her story to tell. I can only tell you what it was like for me: terrifying. It was terrifying because I couldn't relate to her experience. It was terrifying because I didn't know how to fix it. Again. Rational arguments didn't work because there was a disconnect between what she knew and what her body was doing. Her body was pumping adrenaline through her veins in preparation for response to some unseen threat despite her mind knowing there wasn't any danger. I couldn't read Bible verses over her. "Cast all your anxiety on him because he cares for you" is a great verse,[8] but it doesn't apply in situations like this. This kind of anxiety isn't that kind of anxiety.

It was terrifying because I didn't know if this was going to be our new normal. For weeks we had managed to keep this from our five-year-old son. How long should we? How do you describe this to a young child? What do you say? Would Sarah learn to cope with this? Would I learn to be someone different for her? Learn to be the person she now needed?

It was terrifying because all of our pleading with God for sleep, for a respite, for peace, for comfort, seemed to go unanswered. Our prayers over the years for a child were met with silence, and now in this moment of acute need, God seemed silent once again. It was terrifying because I began to give up hope that God even answered prayers.

It was terrifying because I had to preach on Sunday and I didn't know what I would say as I stood in front of God's people.

■　■　■

I had only slept a couple of hours the night before. I showered slowly, letting the warm water baptize me back to life. We were well into a week of nights filled with conversations, tears, card playing, reading. Everything but sleep. We survived from one Sunday to the next. I'm the sole pastor at my church, which meant I had to preach this Sunday, just as I did the last. Sleep or no sleep. I dressed, ate a bagel and a banana, kissed Sarah and Luke good-bye (Sarah was in no condition to get to church), and headed off to church.

It was the third Sunday of Advent. Advent is a time of preparation for the coming of Jesus into the world. It is a looking back to remember that the God of the universe, the one who spoke all things into being and continues to hold all things together, took on flesh and became an infant. But it's also a time of looking forward. A time to ground ourselves that Christ will come again. The third Sunday of Advent is known as Gaudete Sunday. *Gaudete* is the Latin word for "rejoice." Gaudete Sunday is the liturgical shift from adoring the one who came to expecting the one who will come. Christ will come again. So we rejoice. At least we're supposed to.

I was preaching from Luke 1:39–56—the story of Mary visiting her relative Elizabeth. Within the story comes a radical song that grounds the church in what God has done and arouses hope in what God will do: Mary's Magnificat.

> "My soul magnifies the Lord,
>> and my spirit rejoices in God my Savior,
> for he has looked on the humble estate of his servant.
>> For behold, from now on all generations will call
>> me blessed;
> for he who is mighty has done great things for me,
>> and holy is his name.
> And his mercy is for those who fear him
>> from generation to generation.
> He has shown strength with his arm;
>> he has scattered the proud in the thoughts of
>> their hearts;
> he has brought down the mighty from their thrones
>> and exalted those of humble estate;
> he has filled the hungry with good things,
>> and the rich he has sent away empty.
> He has helped his servant Israel,
>> in remembrance of his mercy,
> as he spoke to our fathers,
>> to Abraham and to his offspring forever."[9]

Mary's song rejoices in the God who has seen her, the God who has done great things for her, the God who scatters the proud and exalts the humble, the God of mercy. Central to Mary's song is an understanding of who God is and what God is doing. God is the creator who has entered into a covenant with the descendants of Abraham and is now fulfilling his promises made through the prophets. Mary is caught up in that story. She rejoices because her story is enveloped in the salvation story of Israel.

As I stood in the pulpit, I knew the words but didn't feel the comfort they were supposed to provide. They felt forced. Like a victory cry hollowed out by not actually having anything to be victorious over. But I supposed this was normal. My cynicism told me that much of our faith was a conjured triumphalism. We haven't conquered our demons. We haven't risen above our addictions. We haven't felt the valleys being raised up because we refuse to acknowledge we've ever walked through a real valley.

And so midway through the sermon, I stopped and had one of my most vulnerable moments in the pulpit ever.

Here's what I said, with tears streaming down my face:

I wish we could root ourselves in the knowledge of who God is, what he is doing, and who we are as sons and daughters and all will be well. But sometimes it's unbelievably hard to believe that is true. Many times, in fact. Right now, I'm in a place where I read this passage and it doesn't sound believable. It sounds like some nice thought, but the strong arm of the Lord doesn't seem to be doing anything mighty for me and my family.

A few weeks ago, Sarah and I met with our adoption social worker and were given the bad news that the adoption might take longer than we hoped. Since then, we haven't been sleeping at our house. And because of everything going on in our family, I don't feel like I'm doing a good job here. I feel like my life is being dominated by the tyranny of the urgent. If I'm being honest with you, I don't feel like my feet are underneath me at all. I feel like I'm falling, and I don't feel like I should be doing this right now.

And that's when the voices start. They creep in quietly. They come from the back of my skull, up over the top of my head, and then settle right before my eyes so it isn't just that I hear those voices; I see them. All I can see is what they're saying about me.

- You're not good enough to handle all of this.
- This is your fault. If you were a better husband this wouldn't be happening.
- You're a fraud.
- How can you be a pastor?

And because that's what I see, that's all I can believe.

I read Mary's song today, and I can't relate to any of it. In fact, I feel like these promises and hopes are for someone else, because on a day like today, I wonder if I'm even a child of God.

These voices are my doubts. Every fear, every insecurity, every question I have rages in my gut right now.

I believe that doubts aren't antithetical to faith. But I also believe there is a time, as Dallas Willard says, "to doubt your doubts"[10] and confront them with what we believe. And maybe this is a kind of rejoicing. Maybe rejoicing isn't just an act for when we feel happy and everything is going well. Maybe rejoicing is a defiant act of hope in the face of the forces that seek to kill and destroy.

You want me to believe I am a failure, but I will sing of my God's goodness.

You want me to believe that I can't do this, but I will sing of God's enabling power.

You want me to believe that this situation will define my future, but I will sing of God's mighty deeds.

Holding on to joy is my offensive attack against evil.

So I'm not going to trust what I feel. I'm not going to buy into what the voices are saying. I'm going to rejoice because of what God says. Because despite what I feel or experience, I want what God says to be true.

Looking back on it now, I believe this sermon was the most appropriate sermon I've ever preached on Gaudete Sunday. We can rejoice because Christ will come again. It doesn't always feel like it, but that is our faith. Faith isn't always about what we feel. As David Bentley Hart writes, "To believe in the infinite goodness of being, one must be able to see it; and this no mere argument can bring about."[11]

Faith is about what we choose to see and hold on to. We can hold on to our doubts, but they won't sustain us. It's tempting to hold on to our pain, but pain can't anchor us when the winds blow. It's tempting to only see the suffering in this world because it is legion. Death, anger, doubts, suffering, and pain surround us and overwhelm our five senses, informing us that, beyond a shadow of doubt, they not only exist but define reality. More than resurrection, restoration, reconciliation, relief, and peace, the negative appears more real. To have hope, we have to be able to see the good in the world. Faith is the corrective lenses that allow us to see what we were blinded to. Faith is defiant because it refuses to accept the illusion that tragedy and injustice are the way of the universe, choosing instead to hold tightly to the hope that the central claims of Christianity are the underpinnings of reality: Christ has died; Christ has risen; Christ will come again!

When we're wandering in the darkness, that's the light we walk toward.

# CHAPTER 6

# HOW BEAUTY BLOOMS

## *More Mystery Than You Can Handle*

There is something in us, as storytellers and as listeners to stories, that demands the redemptive act, that demands that what falls at least be offered the chance to be restored.

Flannery O'Connor, *Mystery and Manners*

For a few moments before the room got crowded, our family gathered around my grandfather's casket to say our good-byes. My aunts and uncles slowly came into the room and embraced one another. Gathered in small groups of three or four people, we made our way around the room, looking at flowers and pictures and paying our respects. The now quiet room would soon be filled with conversations, the telling of stories, and even laughter. But for now, it was somber. Words were spoken only with hushed voices and were interrupted by the occasional sniffle as someone was overcome by the moment.

I saw him enter the room and recognized him immediately; he was the grandfather of my childhood friends. His eyes were red, his movements urgent. It was obvious he wanted to be there while simultaneously feeling like he didn't belong. For the life of me, I couldn't figure out why he had come at this time. Why not when everyone else came? Did he know my grandfather well? Why was he so upset? Why had he come so early?

I moved over to my dad.

"Why is June here? Were he and Grandpa friends?"

"You didn't know?" Dad asked me.

"Know what?"

"After Grandma passed, Grandpa heard that June's wife was also dealing with dementia. Grandpa reached out to him and asked if he could take him to coffee and help in any way. They've been meeting weekly ever since."

I was dumbfounded. My grandfather was a great man, but this shocked me. It seemed a bit out of character for him, at least how I knew him. Apparently, something bloomed in Grandpa after caring for my grandmother as she suffered from dementia.

My grandmother was a wonderful woman. If I had to describe her in one word, I would say *hospitable*. Grandma had a way of making people feel welcome and special. I remember many times when we would stay with Grandma and Grandpa while my dad and mom were out of town. Grandma would make my brother and me breakfast every morning. It was nothing like what we got at home before school. She'd start by offering cereal and then toast, and then she'd offer to make eggs—bacon too if we needed it—and just in case we weren't quite feeling full, she might whip up some muffins. It's what Grandma did. And as a sidenote, Grandma could cook. She ruined all of her grandkids. Not one of us will ever be able to eat green Jell-O, chocolate sheet cake, or applesauce and have it taste as good as Grandma's. There is Grandma's, and then there is "Uh, thanks for trying."

I grew up in West Michigan in a small Dutch community. For much of my life, I have been known by others by how they know my family. It was always, "Oh, you're Doc Pyle's son." Or,

"You're Barb Pyle's son." And then there was the, "Oh, Hilda is your Grandma? She helped me pick out clothes." That may sound strange, but for years, Grandma worked at a locally owned department store in the small downtown of Holland, Michigan. Based on the number of times I heard stories of Grandma helping to outfit people I've met, it seems feasible that she dressed half of Holland.

I don't think people went to her because Grandma had a special gift of fashion sense. I think she saw people well. When she looked at them, she saw something they didn't see. And that just manifested itself in her being able to say, "I think this would look great on you."

Dementia took my grandmother's mind, but it never took her personality. One year, Sarah and I visited my grandmother and grandfather in Florida. In the evening, we would sit in the living room and chat about the day and about life. Most of the conversation was with Grandpa since Grandma's mind couldn't keep up. But her gift of hospitality was still there. Every five to ten minutes, she would sit up and cheerfully ask, "Can I get anyone a bowl of ice cream?"

At the time, it was evident Grandpa was growing frustrated with Grandma. He put up with the first six times she asked about ice cream, but after that, he was frustrated. There were times he and Grandma would go to my parents' house for dinner, and, as soon as they arrived, he'd head to the sun porch in the back, just to sit for a few minutes by himself. Watching my grandpa take care of my grandma taught me how tiring it is to care for someone who is forgetting how to take care of themselves.

Grandma had dementia for ten years. And while her memory failed her, Grandpa never did. Over time, the emotional weight of caring for Grandma was evident on Grandpa's face. His disposition got quiet. His eyes were tired. He went out of the house less frequently.

But at the same time, something beautiful began to grow in Grandpa. He was not known to be a particularly patient man, but a slow transformation began to take place, and in the end, he became patient. Without patience, Grandma's repeated questions would have made him crazy (or he would have put on a lot of weight by accepting her every offer of ice cream). His patience with Grandma became patience, thoughtfulness, and compassion toward others too.

Thoughtfulness began to define Grandpa. Our family used to gather for big get-togethers on Sundays for birthdays and other celebrations. As Grandma's condition deteriorated, Grandpa made the decision that he and Grandma would visit with the families individually—with my dad and his family, my uncle and his, and so forth. The reason was that he noticed these visits caused less confusion for Grandma than gathering with the large extended family.

Grandma kept the calendar of birthdays at their house. Every year she'd take the previous year's calendar and transfer all the birthdays, anniversaries, and other important events onto the new calendar. She would send the birthday cards and get the Christmas gifts. Grandpa took over this task, making sure no one was forgotten.

Watching his wife's mind slip away while her body persisted birthed something new in my grandpa. Something beautiful. It didn't happen after the suffering. It didn't happen prior to the struggle. It happened right smack in the middle of the swirling helter-skelter.

This is why June was early to the funeral and why he was filled with grief. Grandpa had walked with him through *his* helter-skelter.

■  ■  ■

The story of Abraham troubles me. Lifted up as the perfect archetype for people of faith, his story is difficult to embrace. For one, God calls Abraham to leave his country, his people, and his father's household.[1] In a transient society like ours, this doesn't seem like a big deal. To an ancient individual like Abraham, chasing after God meant everything must be left behind. Family, yes. But also worldview, security, and religion. Abraham was cutting himself off from his past.

Abraham's response is the precursor to the disciples dropping their nets to follow Jesus. Faith boldly trusts that what lies ahead is better than what lies behind. Faith steps into the unknown hoping for something better. Throughout the Bible, faith looks like brazen foolishness to me. I like to fancy myself a risk-taker, but every time I place myself in Abraham's shoes, I'm not sure I would have set out from my homeland. It's likely I would have tried to negotiate a compromise with God. "How about you make me a great nation right here? We've got resources and people. It's the beginnings of a nation already. No sense in reinventing the wheel and starting over, amiright?"

Which makes the second part of Abraham's story seem insane. After the birth of Abraham's son, Isaac, God calls Abraham to take him to a mountain. There Abraham was to build an altar, bind his son, place him on the altar, and run a knife across his throat as a sacrifice to God. Essentially, God told him, "Kill your son. Kill the hopes and dreams you had for this child. Cut yourself off from your future."[2]

How does one even consider doing this? What drives Abraham to hear that command from God and not run the other way? Is it faith? Or is it fanaticism?

More to the point, what kind of God demands that action as a test of faith? What kind of God forces the choice between the God who promised you an unimaginable legacy or the son you prayed for? Even if it all was a simple test, it is cruel in the highest sense.

All this is true. Our modern sensibilities rightly label the plot points of the story as immoral. It might also be true that modern readers engage the story too literally. That isn't to say we dismiss the story or the weight of it. Nor is this a way of avoiding a text we find repugnant. Rather, it is to say we trust the story as good. Yes, the story has a barbaric element to it. But the story is told with the assumption that we will engage the text with a level of trust that keeps us open to the possibility that something wonderful will be revealed.[3]

From the posture of trust and with a perspective that allows us to see the whole of Abraham's story, we see how faith ought to exist in the wide range of human experiences. From the heights of "I will make your name great" to the depths of "take your son, your only son, whom you love—sacrifice him."[4] I cannot think of two greater extremes. The whole human experience resides between those two poles. Abraham is the model who teaches us that we can trust God in the heights of our joy and in the depths of our unimaginable darkness. God is trustworthy when hope is palpable and when despair is overwhelming.

Abraham's willingness to put the totality of his life in the hands of God is what makes his faith worthy of imitation. Like Abraham, our past does not define our future. And like Abraham, our future can be entrusted to God, even when it seems like the events of our life are contradictory to the goodness we expect of God. Circumstances do not define whether or not we trust. They may inform how we trust—with lament, petition, and doubt— but faith still trusts in the God of redemption and restoration. With this God, faith is trust in the possibility of the impossible.

■ ■ ■

I wonder if Shadrach, Meshach, and Abednego thought they'd end up in the furnace. Surely they didn't think it unimaginable that King Nebuchadnezzar would toss them in the flames, but I wonder if they thought it would really come to that. In their speech to King Nebuchadnezzar, they claimed that God would deliver them from the furnace and the hand of the king.[5] It seems they believed their unshakable faith would result in being spared from heat of the fire.

If we're honest, most of us want a God who will save us from the furnace. Not only do we want a God who will save us from the furnace, but we have a particular understanding of what being saved from the furnace actually is. For most of us, saved from the furnace means we'll never have to get into the furnace to begin with. God, we hope, will miraculously deliver us from ever being exposed to anything tragic, anything chaotic, or anything that causes us pain.

Unfortunately, Scripture paints a different picture. While we want a God who saves *from* the furnace, more often we see God save *through* the furnace. Time and time again, this is how God works. Regardless of the kind of suffering, this is the pattern. The Israelites cry out for liberation from Egypt, but liberation comes by going *through* the Red Sea. David had to learn that God would fight for him by going *through* the battle with Goliath. David also had to learn humility by going *through* repentance of his sins against Uriah and Bathsheba. When Israel needed to be reminded that there is no other god besides God, it is a lesson learned *through* exile. Saul became Paul only by going *through* the Damascus Road incident. Resurrection isn't experienced by avoiding death but by going *through* death.

Sovereignty and omnipotence mean that God *can* save us from the furnace. He could have rescued Shadrach, Meshach, and Abednego before the fire surrounded them. He can put up a hedge around us, like he did for Job, that keeps calamity from our household. He can ensure that our jobs are never taken from us, our children never get sick, and our loved ones never die. God could rescue humanity from its sinful plight in some manner other than Jesus' torturous death on the cross. God rarely deals with suffering and pain through avoidance.

I find myself wondering if something essential to being human would be lost if God completely eliminated suffering. I know that sounds insane. People far and near talk of the world as broken. Sermons and books remind us that the world is not as it should be. The brokenness of the world is not a point that people argue. The evidence is legion. But we rarely talk of the world as it should be outside of purely utopian terms. *Peace, harmony, beauty, perfect*, and *shalom* are tossed around as common descriptors of the world God originally created. This perfect state existed in the past but with the introduction of sin was lost.

Our hope is that it will one day be recovered. What should

be—peace, harmony, beauty, perfection, shalom—is also in the future. It's the day in which God will "wipe every tear from their eyes. There will be no more death or mourning or crying or pain, for the old order of things has passed away."[6] We speak of the lost day that was and the day of hope that is coming as a people confined to the day that is. We are not the people who were, nor are we the people who are coming. We are a people who are be-coming.[7]

I wonder if this pattern—the pattern of struggling through something to become—doesn't go all the way back to Eden. With a little imagination, it isn't hard to find some form of suffering or struggle. It's interesting to note the word God used in the creation narrative: *good*. Not perfect. Good. It seems that even the unblemished paradise had the potential to become.

Adam, the first human according to the creation narrative, was set loose in the garden and tasked with guarding the creation. From what, if not something against which he must struggle? Not only were there undefined threats; it seems entirely possible that Adam gained firsthand knowledge of what was "not good" about creation. Might Adam have understood loneliness? Loneliness is a recognition of incompleteness. It's a lack of the presence of others. It is to suffer in the void of relationship. Adam struggled against what was not good in the garden, and it's through his suffering that he cries out in elation when he meets the "bone of [his] bones and flesh of [his] flesh."[8]

In the garden, the man and the woman are faced with limitations. They do not have the knowledge of good and evil. There is a tree they cannot eat from. These limitations are the origins of temptation. Aware of their creaturely condition, the man and the woman begin to experience a kind of anxiety. Why shouldn't we know good from evil? Why would God want to keep that from us? Why must we always be dependent on God? To be anxious is to suffer the onslaught of a thousand questions. I wonder if this kind of suffering existed in the garden—in that place we so often picture as free of struggle?

From the beginning, creation was incomplete. There is a progressive unfolding to God's world. As theologian Terence Fretheim writes, "This potential of becoming is built into the very structures of the world."[9] The world was good. Our struggle and work would make it better.

The symbolic presence of a certain kind of suffering in the garden unlocks a truth we'd rather overlook: to be human is to suffer. That was the design from the beginning. More than that, suffering is a part of the authentic human life. Humans have never passively enjoyed the fruits of the world. We become active participants in our own lives when we wrestle against our limitations and withstand temptations. We drink deeply of relationships after knowing the drought of loneliness. We exhale in peace after the storm of anxiety. Life isn't simply provided. We wring life from our experiences, while at the same time our experiences wring us out from our lives. We are becoming. And our experiences are a part of that process. Without our experiences, we would not be us.

Struggle is at the center of be-coming. Jacob becomes Israel through wrestling with the angel.[10] Jesus becomes the exalted one through the struggle to be obedient at the cross.[11] As Douglas John Hall notices, "Life without any kind of suffering would be no life at all; it would be a form of death. Life—the life of the spirit like the life of the body—depends in some mysterious way upon the struggle to be."[12]

Let's be clear. This isn't some masochistic manifesto glorying in suffering. We shouldn't orient our lives around seeking suffering and then rejoicing in it as if it is a blessing. Nor is this an argument in defense of every form of suffering. Sin's destruction divorces suffering from the process of becoming. Sin is the gale-force winds of *tohu wabohu* rattling the created order, distorting what God intended. What was designed to make us wise, noble, and compassionate has been perverted and threatens to isolate us, consume us, and dehumanize us. To fulfill its design to aid in the process of be-coming, suffering must be redeemed. Any goodness derived from its suffering must come from something that transcends it and orders its chaotic elements into something beautiful.

After Eden, suffering isn't innately redemptive. But our God is redeeming all things, even suffering. A day is coming when God will eliminate suffering and wipe every tear from every eye, but not yet. Until then, it seems that God won't eliminate suffering. We can't count on being saved from the furnace, but we can count on being saved as we endure the furnace. Suffering, even that which sin intended for evil, becomes something that God will use for good. This is the hope of redemption.

■  ■  ■

To this day, I have no idea why we've had to go through infertility, ectopic pregnancy, and anxiety-riddled, sleepless nights. Like everyone who has ever suffered, I've searched for meaning. What did we do to deserve this? What are we supposed to learn from this? How does this fit into God's grand plan for the universe? Any explanation offered to these largely existential questions seem trite. As much as I desire some answer to my questions, I've come to believe that my desire will go unsatisfied.

After Job lost everything, he spent thirty-seven chapters demanding an explanation from God for his suffering. When God finally speaks, God extols the complexity of the world. God doesn't simply remind Job of God's power to subjugate creation to his will, but he reveals how that power is coupled with a joy-filled relationship to creation. God laid the foundation of the earth, and the morning stars and angels shouted for joy. God forms the sea and its boundaries, not through an impersonal show of strength but relationally in a conversation with the sea. And when the seas were formed, they did not simply appear, but they "burst forth from the womb" like a mother giving birth to a child.[13] God's speech to Job is filled with relational language and imagery so that Job might know the nature of God's power.

Philosopher Eleonore Stump writes, "God deals as a parent with his creatures, from the sea and rain to the raven and the donkey and even the monstrous behemoth and leviathan. He brings them out of the womb, swaddles, feeds, and guides them, and even plays with them. Most importantly, he talks to them; and somehow, in some sense or other, they talk to him in return."[14]

God is all-powerful and sovereign, but he does not wield infinite power to subjugate his creation to his will. Instead God nurtures relationships.

And yet God never answers Job's questions. Not in any direct way. I take that to mean that sometimes bad things happen without an explanation that will satisfy us. I wonder how Job would have experienced his suffering had God explained—*prior to* the tragedy—the conversation between God and Satan in the divine throne room. Would Job have passively endured? Would he have simply waited for the resolution he knew was coming? Would the flourishing at the end of the story have been as sweet? I doubt it. In fact, I think the explanation would have cheapened the experience. As I tried to put myself in Job's place, had God let me in on the conversation with Satan and the plan, I would have felt like a prop. Resentment would demand that God find another way to play the game with Satan.

What about an explanation *after* we've endured difficult circumstances? Would that soothe our troubled minds? Perhaps. But we should ask *whose* troubled mind. Ours as the one who suffered, or ours as the observer of suffering? For a child who undergoes chemotherapy for leukemia, the comfort from a parent is more important than the explanation of why their child must endure nausea and hair loss and needle poke after needle poke. What is most meaningful is knowing that their mother loves them. To the observer, we want an explanation as to why the mother is allowing the child to suffer. What justifies the mother's willingness to let her child suffer? Will the child be in a better place after suffering? These explanations are necessary for us, the observer, to accept that the mother truly loves her child. The child doesn't need the explanation; the child needs the experience of the mother's love. That's enough.[15]

In fact, the majority of Job's story is one of Job rejecting his friends' theories about why tragedy fell on his household. Job refuses to accept the loss of his property, the death of his children, and the boils on his body as good simply because God allowed them. Instead, Job indicts God, claiming that God is supposedly good, and therefore what has happened to him deserves some recourse. Job's relentless commitment to the goodness of God appalls his friends. As Stump points out, "The comforters are shocked that Job refuses simply to take as good anything done by God. But Job is shocked by them and their willingness to abandon any objective standard of goodness in the interest of being on the side of the ruler of the universe."[16] This isn't to say that Job rejects God. Rather, as Stump adds, it is that "Job takes his stand with the goodness of God, rather than with the office of God as ruler of the universe."[17]

Our quickness to try to make sense of suffering betrays an anxiety about the world we live in. Randomness is terrifying. It doesn't matter if it is perceived or real. The chaotic nature of a sin-filled world is deeply unsettling, so we invent countless theories to bring a modicum of order to what we do not understand. Answers to human suffering will always be inadequate. We'd do well to remember that even God doesn't respond to suffering with an explanation. To further condemn any inclination to provide reasons for our suffering, remember that God did not hold Job in contempt for his indignation. Surprisingly, God rebuked those whose theology was most sanitized, who kowtowed to God and his office, who prodded Job to simply accept the events as appropriate because God is God and Job is not. To those people God said, "My anger burns against you and against your two friends, for you have not spoken of me what is right, as my servant Job has."[18]

Job realizes the most important thing isn't what God said to him. Preachers have often missed this point, choosing instead to use God's words against Job. Claiming God silenced Job by reminding him that Job is not God, preachers effectively exhort us to silence and passivity in our situations. This misses the point of the whole book. The point isn't what God says to Job. The point is that God says anything to Job at all! The point isn't what God says in response to suffering, but *where God is.* God is present. Face-to-face with Job. What Job knew in the theoretical he was now experiencing. This is why Job exclaims, "My ears had heard of you but now my eyes have seen you."[19]

On top of that, it seems that God isn't interested in providing answers to our questions. God could have given Job an answer to his questions. God could have explained the conversation between God and Satan. God chooses not to. Which seems to be how God operates with us. Despite our most fervent cries for an explanation, God is often silent. That isn't to say that God doesn't bring about something good from tragedy. That's the heartbeat of redemption. But redemption isn't an explanation for why we had to suffer.

Take the story of Shadrach, Meshach, and Abednego. After refusing to worship the idol set up by King Nebuchadnezzar, these three men were thrown into the white-hot furnace.[20] As the story goes, they walked out of the furnace not even smelling like smoke. I remember this story from Sunday school flannelgraphs. The moral of the story was always about faith. "Faith will save us" was hammered into us to the back of our skulls.

I was never taught the words that Shadrach, Meshach, and Abednego said prior to being thrown in the furnace: "The God we serve is able to deliver us . . . and he will deliver us . . . But even if he does not . . ."[21] These words are dangerous. Because what if God doesn't? What if God doesn't bring restoration in my marriage? What if God doesn't grab the attention of my wayward daughter who is making poor choices? What if God doesn't fix our financial difficulties? Will I still have faith? Most of us are handed down a faith that doesn't have room for the "but even if he does not," because saying that would imply doubts.

Only when our trust in God's goodness becomes independent of what God does for us individually can we have a faith that says, "Our God can and our God will, but even if he doesn't." But that doesn't come easy. Getting there requires a shift in our expectations and understandings of how God works for our good.

Because maybe that story isn't about Shadrach, Meshach, and Abednego's faith at all. Maybe the point of the whole story is to direct our attention to the faithfulness of the one who meets them in the furnace. Maybe the miracle is that we pay attention enough to notice that God is with us.

■ ■ ■

Isaiah prophesies about a God-man who will inhabit the helter-skelter. He is the Messiah—the one who would rescue Israel from her enemies. But rather than declaring that this Messiah will defeat Israel's enemies with power and strength, Isaiah startles his listeners by prophesying that the Servant of the Lord will face suffering, humiliation, and loss. Salvation will not come by the arm of the Lord crushing the enemy. Salvation comes when the enemy crushes the Servant. This is why Isaiah can write, "He was despised and rejected by mankind, a man of suffering, and familiar with pain."[22]

Jesus is this "man of suffering"—this man of sorrows.

This statement is more profound than it is simple. It reminds us of the profound mystery of the incarnation. The fullness of God dwelled in the person of Jesus. Jesus is the "visible image of the invisible God."[23] He was "with God in the beginning" of creation, and "all things were made" through him.[24] The laws of the world that we depend on—gravity, inertia, thermal dynamics, and opposites attracting—are sustained by his right hand. He is the God who left behind the riches of heaven and became poor so that we might be made rich.[25]

As the apostle John writes, "the Word became flesh."[26] God became human and, like us, got dirt under his fingernails, dust in his eyes, pangs of hunger in the morning, and a tongue thick with thirst. He also wept. Overcome by the weight of the broken world, he cried out to God that he would be spared from suffering. As the great preacher Charles Spurgeon notes, Jesus was not a sorrowful man, but a man of sorrows. It was a peculiarity of his countenance:

> We might well call Him, "A man of holiness," for there was no fault in Him. Or "A Man of labors," for He did His Father's business earnestly. Or, "A Man of eloquence," for never man spoke like this Man. We might right fittingly call Him in the language of our hymn, "The Man of Love," for never was there greater love than glowed in His heart. Still, conspicuous as all these and many other excellences were, yet had we gazed upon Christ, and been asked afterwards what was the most striking peculiarity in Him, we should have said His sorrows.[27]

In the incarnation of Jesus, God identifies with our sorrows. God is not far-off and distant; he is with us in the muck and mire of life. Suffering is not foreign to him—something that God knows about only by omniscience. In Jesus, God was intimate with grief and the salty taste of tears. Jesus is in the furnace with us, just as he was with Shadrach, Meshach, and Abednego.

The Son of Man had to suffer, not only to dismantle the power of death, but also to fully identify with humanity. Salvation came through suffering.

This is a love that is more than we can handle. Our God becomes human and meets us in the most common human experience. Precisely when it feels like our humanity has been taken from us, God finds us in the chaos and restores it to us.

There's hope in this love. God's love doesn't eliminate our suffering. God will not take away our struggle of be-coming. Instead, God's love is his refusal to leave us alone. Blessed are those who mourn, for they will be comforted by the palpable presence of God. Immanuel—God with us. And perhaps that gives us just enough strength to continue on. Perhaps we can embrace our inability to control, fix, or change our situations— and lament. Lament is the ultimate display of trust in God's ability to right the wrong of the world.

That said, nothing in life is certain, certainly not the outcome of suffering. God has not given us a guarantee about how he will use or redeem our suffering. We cannot place our trust in a particular outcome. All we are assured of is that God will be with us. As we sit in the ashes of our grief, Jesus will be next to us. Which is where he has been all along. Jesus is waiting for us at the end of our capacities. This is why the Teacher of Ecclesiastes writes, "It is better to go to a house of mourning than to go to a house of feasting."[28]

Tucked into a rarely read passage in the Old Testament is a story of the ark of the covenant as it enters Solomon's temple. The ark was believed to be the resting place for the presence of God, and so it was placed in the center of the temple in the Most Holy Place. This small room was dark every day of the year. And so

Solomon, at the dedication of the temple, said, "The LORD has said that he would dwell in thick darkness."[29]

What separated the Most Holy Place from the temples of other gods was that there was no image of God. There wasn't a statue, a picture, or an idol of any kind. The room was devoid of any image of God and of light every day of the year. Except one. On that day, Yom Kippur, the high priest would go into the Most Holy Place. On that day, there was an image of God in the form of an image bearer who went into the presence of God, who dwelled in darkness.[30]

No longer does God dwell behind the curtain of the Most Holy Place. When Jesus took his last breath on the cross, the curtain was torn in two, and the dividing wall between God and the world was destroyed.[31] God doesn't dwell in the darkness of a private sanctuary in the middle of a grand temple; God dwells in the darkness of our lives. In the pain and suffering, in the confusion and chaos, in the violence and tragedy—God is there in the oppressive darkness that surrounds us. As John wrote in his gospel, "The light shines in the darkness."

The light shines in my darkness.

The light shines in the darkness, and the darkness could not overcome it.[32]

Trusting that God will be with us in our most difficult trials makes it possible for us to embrace our lived life—the good and the bad, the easy and the difficult, the joyful and the tearful. Our ability to be fully present to the pain inflicted by this world is mysteriously linked to our ability to be fully present to the beauty of this world. Much of our life is spent pursuing one without the other, but this is a fool's errand. Frederick Buechner poignantly captures this in his book *Lion Country* after the main character, Antonio, loses his sister to a bone disorder:

When Miriam's bones were breaking, for instance, if I could have pushed a button that would have stopped not her pain but the pain of her in me, I would not have pushed the button because, to put it quite simply, my pain was because I loved her, and to have wished my pain away would have been somehow to wish my love away as well. And at my best and bravest I do not want to escape the future either, even though I know that it contains what will someday be my own great and final pain. Because a distaste for dying is twin to a taste for living, and again I don't think you can tamper with one without somehow doing mischief to the other. But this is at my best and bravest.[33]

God's intent is that we will have life abundantly. In the darkness, we see what truly shines. During birthdays and weddings and bluebird picnics we don't truly understand how bright those events are. Without the darkness, those events simply fade into the sunny backdrop of every other moment. The best things in life wouldn't be the best without the worst. Which leaves us with a sobering truth: the best life isn't the pain-free life; the best life is when every moment is fully lived. That's the abundant life. That's the life that is more than we can handle.

# CHAPTER 7

# EYES OPENED
## *More Empathy Than You Can Handle*

The questions which one asks oneself begin, at least, to illuminate the world, and become one's key to the experience of others.

James Baldwin, *Nobody Knows My Name*

Jairus and Rudina lived in Beit Sahour, a small town just outside of Bethlehem. Bethlehem is in the West Bank of modern-day Palestine, on the other side of the wall dividing Palestine from Israel. This young Palestinian Christian couple graciously opened their home to two young American seminarians for a couple of days. I was one of them.

Their home was a two-bedroom apartment on the first floor of their building. The main room was a large square. There were no walls separating the living space from the kitchen and dining room. White tiles and white walls made the room feel bright and open. The walls were bare except for a wooden cross and a few small photos spread around the room. Centered in the room was a couch and a chair. Both faced the wall where a TV stood on a stand.

Rudina took us to what would be our bedroom. Once again, white tile floors and white walls. Two twin beds and a dresser filled the small space. Without hesitation, my seminary companion, Mark, called the bed with the Garfield the Cat comforter.

Their daughter, Ludra, was perhaps the most beautiful child I have ever seen. Maybe two years old, she had silky black hair with loose curls and the deepest, blackest eyes that sparkled incessantly like a clear, crisp October night.

Over the course of our time with them, Jairus and Rudina shared their lives with us. One night we ate ka'ak, a ring of sesame-crusted bread, with Rudina's family. We broke bread around a small table in their apartment, dipping it into a bowl of olive oil and spices. As we left, Rudina's father told me it was too cold for me to go outside without a proper jacket. (It was January and about 40 degrees. I'm from Michigan, so this was practically shorts weather.) He grabbed his black scarf and wrapped it around my neck. Then he patted me on my chest with his palm and said something in Arabic.

"He wants you to have it," Rudina said.

"Tell him thank you," I said, overwhelmed. Not by the gift of the scarf. By these people. The unwavering hospitality that continually welcomed me, invited me to the table, and offered something to me, a stranger, was unlike anything I expected to experience. I was entranced but also puzzled. The United States news media had instilled in me the notion that Palestinians were terrorists who could not be trusted. I was led to believe they were uncivil and incendiary. Their refusal to recognize the nation of Israel was evidence of their deficient humanity. But my time with this family was richly infused with warmth, kindness, and hospitality. The dominant narrative began to unravel. I was no longer seeing the narrative; I was seeing the people.

The next night, we visited with Jairus's family. They lived across town in a ground-level apartment. The building was on a hillside along a shallow valley. On the opposite hill, an Israeli military outpost had imposed itself on the landscape, with its massive walls, barbed wire fences, and bright lights illuminating the surrounding area—all in the name of protection from the Palestinians.

There was less food than at Rudina's family's house but much more music. Jairus's family was loud and excitable. A radio blasted Arabic dance music. Mark and I were pulled to our feet as the family clapped and shouted at the crazy Americans who were now dancing in their tiny living room. Out came the hubbly bubbly—otherwise known as a hookah, the traditional water pipe used to smoke flavored tobacco. The room became filled with sweet, apple-scented smoke. Laughter joined the haze and hovered over us like the Spirit of God over the waters of the deep. It was a multisensory textured haze. The cloud of holy humanity that enveloped us overstimulated the room that was already struggling to contain this vivacious Palestinian family and their two dancing Dutch-American visitors.

After a bit, Jairus motioned to us.

"Come."

Mark and I followed him to a wall in the family room. He began moving pictures to reveal holes on the wall. The holes were about the size of a pinky finger and looked like someone had gotten carried away with a drill.

"Bullets," Jairus told us.

We asked Rudina to come over, since Jairus's English wasn't good and our Arabic was worse. She explained that the holes were from bullets shot randomly into the neighborhood by the military outpost on the other hill. My mouth opened as I listened, horrified at what I was hearing. This family, so boisterous and fun-loving, were dancing amid the constant anxiety of a stray bullet finding its way into their house. How could they laugh when at any moment their joy could be turned to sorrow?

These people, who are often painted as barbaric, aren't so different from us. We may feel more removed from the precariousness of life, but are we really farther away from tragedy? A drunk driver who runs a red light. A doctor's mouth forming the word *cancer*. A madman entering a school with assault rifles. We may not live with visible reminders of life's fragility adorning our walls, but our joy can be stolen just as quickly. Life isn't guaranteed. We know that viscerally, but we work hard to shelter ourselves from this kind of chaos. Here there was no spackle to cover the holes. The precariousness of life hung like a framed picture for all to reflect on.

Maybe that's why the music was loud and they danced so freely. Because tonight they could dance. Tomorrow? That wasn't guaranteed.

That night, I began to see that we, Americans and Palestinians, aren't that different. I don't want to erase our strong cultural distinctions. I'm not minimizing the extreme situation Palestinians experience by equating my suburban existence to their life behind the wall. Yes, there are significant differences. But our basic human needs and wants are the same. We all are shaped by the same desires—security, a future, family, belonging, hope.

As time has passed, I've come to understand the universality of our hearts' desires. It's true of Syrian families asking for refuge in the West. It's true of black Americans asking us to take a hard look at police brutality. It's true of LGBTQ individuals who plead with the church to acknowledge the pain they've felt as they hear callous idioms like "love the sinner, hate the sin." We all want the same thing—the possibility of *flourishing*.

The next morning, I sat on the couch in Rudina and Jairus's living room. Rudina came over, handed me Ludra, and dropped into a chair across from me. We made small talk about our sleep and the day ahead of us. Still unsettled by my time with their family the previous night, I asked her, "How do you deal with all of this? With the wall and the bullet holes and the checkpoints?"

"It's hard," she said, "but we manage."

She looked down at the floor. I misread the cue to mean that the conversation was over. But Rudina was just collecting herself.

She reclaimed my gaze. "What do you think we Palestinians deserve?" she asked.

Now it was my turn to study the floor. I had never *really* understood the conflict between Israel and Palestine. I still don't. But I was beginning to see it differently. The news media may give us some of the facts, but we cannot even begin to understand the human element behind the facts until we've sat at someone's table or danced in their house or been entrusted with holding their little children.

■ ■ ■

January winds in Indiana are brutal. The winds whip snow and cold against houses as if they are mad. After a long day of Sunday activities, Sarah and I sat on the floor and lit a fire in the fireplace to protect against the bullying winds outside the window.

The phone rang. Sarah answered, and her eyes widened as she listened to the person on the other end. It was the adoption agency. We had been matched. A mother in Florida had chosen us to be the parents of her soon-to-be-born child.

Considering the massive nature of what was taking place,

it was disconcerting how short the phone call was. One would think that a life-altering event like a child being placed with your family would require a conversation that lasted for hours. With pregnancy, you have nine months to prepare for a child. Shouldn't there be something comparable for this moment? Instead, you get a short phone call telling you there will be an infant in your house in six weeks: *Congratulations. You've been matched with a baby [insert gender] expected on [insert due date]. Talk it over and confirm with us as soon as possible that you'll accept this child.*

Actually, our conversation was a bit longer. And it wasn't just about being matched and getting ready to receive a child. Included was this exchange:

**Agency:** One more thing. The child is African American, and he's a boy. Are you okay with that?

**Sarah:** Yes. Why?

**Agency:** Because the birth mother chose another family first, but when that family found out it was a black boy, they turned down the match. The birth mother wants to be sure you're okay with adopting a black boy.

It didn't dawn on me at the time, but I later came to realize that white families may feel uncomfortable adopting a black child—particularly a black boy—at this time in history. For the last couple of years, American news outlets have reported incident after tragic incident of black men being shot or victimized by racial profiling by police officers. Social media feeds have been filled with live videos, photos, and stories of violence against black men. Eric Garner. Michael Brown. John Crawford III. Tamir Rice. Stephon Clark. President Barack Obama echoed the thoughts of many parents of black boys when he said, after Trayvon Martin was shot, "This could have been my son."

For a long time, Americans have been able to pretend that racial tensions were a thing of the past. But the omnipresence of cell phone cameras has exposed what we've long tried to ignore. We are not a postracial society. For some prospective adoptive parents, entering the tension and perhaps confronting their own biases may be more than they can handle.

Sarah hung up the phone and told me the few details she was given. Two years of waiting. Two years of wondering if this moment would come. Now, if we were to say yes, we'd have a baby in six weeks. No matter how long one has had to wait, processing the enormity of that moment is impossible.

"This is it," I said.

"Are you sure?" she asked.

"Absolutely."

From the very beginning we had said the race of the child would not matter. We would adopt this child. And we would embrace whatever complexities and learning accompanied a transracial adoption.

■  ■  ■

I grew up in a historically Dutch Reformed community on the west side of Michigan. I knew a black kid growing up. One. I met him in middle school. His family lived across the street from my great-grandmother. When we would visit her, we would some-times go over to his house and jump on their trampoline. A few times he came over to my house. In high school, our circle of friends changed and we rarely talked.

I went to a small Christian liberal arts college. None of my friends were black. Truth be told, none of my friends were anything other than white.

When I was thirty-five, I went to a writers conference to try to learn the craft of writing. (I had a book deal, so I figured this would be beneficial.) Before the dinner break, I gathered with friends from the online world to find a place to eat. We set a destination and piled into cars. Of course, every restaurant was packed, so our large group split into smaller groups. I found myself with three others—all of them African American. Just before my food arrived, it dawned on me: this was the first time I had ever been a minority. In any group. Anywhere. Again, I was thirty-five.

The realization didn't make me uncomfortable at dinner, but it did make me mindful. In a way I'd never realized before, I found myself considering every word I said, how I said it, and what my words and tone might convey. I didn't get some of their jokes. I didn't understand some of the things being talked about. I felt like an outsider.

Later, reflecting on that dinner, I wondered whether this was just the tiniest taste of how people of color may feel in a predominately white society. How they may have to translate their words to fit the culture. How they may not understand or like every joke. How they may feel like an outsider. A one-hour dinner began to shift my understanding about race in America. Not to say that I understand now, because the lived experience of people of color in America will always be impossible for me as a white man to fully understand. Rather, I began to wake up to all that I don't understand.

For much of my life, I've lived in privileged ignorance of the reality of being black in America. I knew some of the history of Martin Luther King Jr. and the civil rights movement, and I had read a few of King's speeches, but by and large, I was oblivious to the experience of my black and brown neighbors. But now I was going to have a black child. So I began to consume books. I started to ask questions and listen. I engaged podcasts as conversation partners. I felt it was my responsibility as a parent and as a Christian—to learn to love my neighbor as myself.

It became clear I didn't know history as well as I thought. I didn't know about Reconstruction Era politics. I was aghast to learn how common lynchings were at the turn of the century, not to mention how rarely the perpetrators were prosecuted. The racial component of the GI Bill for returning World War II veterans was news to me. Lending practices, housing ordinances, voting requirements, incarceration rates—I was overwhelmed by how much history I didn't know.

It wasn't just history. My wife and I sought out our African American friends, websites, Facebook groups, and YouTube videos to learn new approaches to skin and hair care. My wife teaches dance, and she found out that it wasn't until a couple of years ago that skin-toned tights for black dancers were made available. Prior to that, black dancers had to buy nude leggings and dye them. We found out we didn't know what we didn't know. Privilege looks like not having to know those things because our world is tailored for us. As middle-class, white Protestants, we were at the center.

My eyes started to open to a different kind of suffering—a suffering I'd been oblivious to—the collective suffering endured by a people over a prolonged period of time.

This *tohu wabohu* has swirled for centuries and, in an insidious and diabolical scheme, sustains its helter-skelter by creating an alternate order to the just and harmonious order of God. For those of us who have not directly suffered under those systems and structures, we must, like Job's friends for the first seven days,[1] sit in silence and listen. We need to build our capacity to empathize with those whose experiences are not our experiences. To see the world from their perspective. There we may began to see that there isn't one reality; there are many realities. A world that works for me may not work for another. We may find that the rules of the game aren't the same for everyone. One person may be able to pull themselves up by their bootstraps, but another may not even have a boot.[2]

Empathy subverts the systems and structures of oppression. However, these same systems and structures that oppress one people group often induce an impoverishment of empathy in another group. That impoverishment deems listening to another as unnecessary. Instead, explanations for God's actions or justifications for the way things are from our position of comfort within the system are offered instead of empathy.

Where systems of oppression are present, everyone suffers. Some suffer the indignity of being seen as less than human. Some struggle on the margins of society to belong. Still others live with the unspoken message that their very bodies are expendable. Those in the dominant group at the center of society suffer too. By being cut off from their fellow humans, those at the center fail to see the wonder and beauty that is the image of God in all people. Judgmentalism, indifference, and callousness invade hearts and minds. In the end, a part of their humanity shrivels as people are treated as other.

I realize many readers will be exasperated that we're talking about race and systemic sin. After all, this is a book about finding God when life feels as if it's more than we can handle. It's not about racism. This idea is not lost on me. And yet God's grace toward us is often experienced in the listening ear of another. Empathy connects us not only with others but also with God. In our most difficult moments we want someone to say, "I see you. I hear you. I'm with you." As we seek to follow Jesus' command to love our neighbor as ourselves, we embrace the task of learning to be empathetic.

Perhaps the biggest killer of empathy is comparison. We place our suffering on a scale alongside another person's suffering to determine who gets the right to talk about their pain. Did you lose a job, or do you have cancer? At least you have your health—so stop complaining. The person with cancer gets to talk. Is your child rebelling, or did your spouse cheat on you? Did you lose your spouse, or have you experienced the generational trauma of being seen as other?

Suffering is not a sport with a winner and a loser. Pain is pain, regardless of its source. Making judgments about the intensity with which another experiences pain is a form of cruel indifference. Loving others well begins with listening well. Rushing to explanation or dismissal is to assume the role of Job's friends.

So we lay down our preconceived ideas, our established worldviews, our partisan political affiliations, and our defense mechanisms in order to listen and learn from those who experience the world differently. Listening, learning, and empathizing are not more than we can handle. They're precisely what we as Christians are called to do in the face of an overwhelming world.

■ ■ ■

We have yet to ask the question, "What is suffering?" We should not take for granted that we all think about suffering in the same way. It's likely there is a different definition for every person who reads this book. How, then, do we know when we are suffering? What constitutes suffering?

I would say my friends Jairus and Rudina suffer. But their suffering doesn't look anything like what my wife and I experienced with the ectopic pregnancy. Our suffering was caused by an acute circumstance. For my wife, there was physical pain involved in the suffering. Pain is often a sign that suffering is present, but not always. Athletes often feel physical pain as they train, but we wouldn't say they suffer. If suffering required physical pain, it would negate a lot of legitimate suffering that is mental.

We also know that people can suffer emotionally and spiritually. Faithful followers of Jesus are often haunted by the dark night of the soul—that wilderness journey where God seems far off, our faith flaccid, and our ability to "fix it" futile.

Jairus's and Rudina's suffering was connected to an ongoing, chronic situation. Their suffering belonged to the collective suffering of a people. In our highly individualized First World context, many of us are removed from this kind of suffering. Unless we belong to a minority group. African Americans, Native Americans, those below or near the poverty line, and the LGBTQ community are all groups of people who suffer both as individuals and collectively.

One way to think of suffering is to see it as an impediment to flourishing. Philosopher Eleonore Stump examines this idea in her book *Wandering in the Darkness* when she writes that suffering "diminishes her and makes her less than the flourishing self she would be if she were to flourish. It makes her less than she ought to be—that is, less than she would be if the world were what it ought to be."[3]

To see suffering only through the lens of individual pain brought about by tragic circumstances misses the quiet, daily, systemic millstones endured by many. Anything that makes another less than human is evil. And to be made less than human is to suffer. Every person is created in the image of God. What made the Garden of Eden so good was that it was designed for the *flourishing* of creation, including the image-bearing humans. Even the struggle that existed in the garden, as we noted in the last chapter, existed to help us flourish.

The Hebrews called this *shalom*. Shalom is a kind of peace. Harmony is another word for it. It happens when the world functions as it was designed to function. If we pay attention, we can catch glimpses of it out of the corner of our eyes. When my children play with one another without fighting—chasing each other around the house, giggling, and enjoying each other's presence—I find myself overwhelmed with a sense of harmony because that's how it's supposed to be.

It's those nights when you sit with good friends and good food and good drink and everyone enjoys each other's presence. When the stories and the conversation are as rich as the fare on the table. When the meal extends long into the night because no one wants to get up and leave the table. In those moments, if you were to back away from the table long enough to hear the quiet hum reverberating in your bones, you might hear, *This is how it's supposed to be*. And it is.

That feeling gets at the idea of flourishing. Every human being longs to flourish. We may imagine different specifics when we talk of flourishing, but the sentiment—this is how it is supposed to be—is something we all long for. One way to define suffering could be this: suffering exists when our flourishing is undermined or stolen from us by natural circumstances, systemic injustices, poor choices, or any combination thereof.

Jairus and Rudina, my wife and I, you and yours—we all have the same desires for our families. We may be separated by thousands of miles. Our situations may be worlds apart—so vastly different. But the desires of our hearts are the same: family, food, security, a future for our children. The details may differ, but the beat of our hearts is the same. We long to flourish. And we suffer when this desire to flourish goes unmet.

■　■　■

A conversation about flourishing requires a conversation about what impedes it: sin.

Western Christianity does not have a robust theology of sin. Typical understandings frame sin as an individual's infractions against God's commands. Guilt, then, belongs to the person. Collective guilt is not just a foreign idea; it's resisted.

Americans do not readily welcome the idea that we are complicit in sinful systems. For many, the idea that we may be complicit in a corporate sin we are not directly responsible for seems unfair. It's why so many white Americans buck against any claims of systemic racism by arguing that it's a heart issue. Or why abortion is framed as an individual right rather than a systemic evil connected to poverty, access to health care, or liberal sexual practice. Or why patriarchy is still supported by so many churches (under the guise of different terms), despite its structural subjugation of women. Our individual understanding of sin provides little framework for comprehending systemic realities affecting our neighbors of differing ethnicities, religions, genders, and sexual orientations.

Learning that I would be the father of a black child caused me to take a hard look at the systemic realities separating the white and black experience of America and the American Dream.

I began to learn that for most of America's history, segregation was encouraged through racially driven policies of federal, state, and local governments. The war on drugs that started in the 1970s incarcerates black Americans at a rate significantly higher than white Americans, even though blacks and whites use drugs at very similar rates.[4] Black Americans are more likely to be profiled by police[5] and are "more than six times as likely as whites to be sentenced to prison for *identical* crimes."[6]

These are just a few of the sinful systems that exist in America. As Americans, we are complicit in their existence. No, we didn't create them. You may have never uttered a racist word in your life. But the systems exist on our watch. As image bearers of God responsible for helping the world flourish, we have a responsibility to wage a battle against "the powers of this dark world."[7] Without a robust theology of sin, we will not see any need to repent of these systems.

America's rugged individualism has gutted our collective theology of sin. But it's not just sin that's understood to be specific to the individual. Even our beliefs about flourishing are individualistic. Flourishing in the world, according to the American myth, is dependent on the hard work and good choices of each person.

History is unimportant. It doesn't matter that while some black people's ancestors were enslaved, white people's ancestors were given land in the Homestead Act. It doesn't matter that white veterans of World War II were given loans for mortgages while banks refused to give loans to black veterans. We perpetuate the axiom that everyone has the same opportunity in America—the white boy born as an heir to generational wealth and the black boy born as an heir to generational poverty. The American myth claims they have equal opportunity.

My learning revealed that the American Dream of climbing the socioeconomic ladder unintentionally gave many of us a myopic, self-centered view of the world—myself included. Perhaps even subconsciously, we began to think, *As long as we're doing well—and as long as those we really love are doing well—then the world works. Government, politics, economics, the legal system, law enforcement, distribution of wealth, the schools are all fine. We make this determination as long as these things continue to benefit us. If the structure of society works for us, then it must be able to work for everyone. All* they *have to do is share our thoughts, our values, and especially our work ethic to flourish as we do. If they can't or if they are suffering in a society that we can flourish in, well, that must be on them.*

This preoccupation with individual success and triumph translated to an individual understanding of suffering. Upon that foundation, it becomes difficult to accept that systems and structures oppressing entire people groups are the powers of this dark world in our day. I was never forced to look at the power structures of the world until I was faced with the possibility of being the father of a child of another race. I had to admit that my older son would have a different experience of the world than the child we would adopt. Our firstborn son wouldn't hear racist terms in school said about him. His relationship with authorities would be different. People in stores would make different assumptions about him as he carried toys up and down the aisles. The moment I considered these possibilities was the moment I began to empathize with people whose experience of this world is different than mine.

Admittedly, this is hard. It can feel like more than we can handle. It's easier to see the world through an individualistic lens. The world is reduced to "if you do $x$, then $y$." The cause and effect is clear. Cause-and-effect thinking is logical. Simple even. Systems thinking is difficult and messy. There are too many factors to consider. Too many things outside of our control. So we don't talk about principalities and powers in a systemic sense. Instead, we perpetuate the idea that principalities and powers are the spiritual forces that attack individuals. They bring suffering and frustration in the form of cancer, anger, sickness, and maybe lousy parking spots at Target. These individual spirits can be triumphed over with the right kind of faith.

It has taken me a long time to accept the fact that my individual sins of greed, selfishness, prejudice, tribalism, and lust are not isolated from yours. As much as I wish my sins only affected me and those I directly interact with, they don't. They twist and concoct, mix and morph, combine and grow, into something bigger than an individual act.

In 2015, I traveled with World Vision to document the work they were doing in Cambodia. One day, as we drove back to the capital city of Phnom Penh from the countryside, we passed a massive line of factories. Filing out of the factories and filling the streets were huge flatbed trucks. The trucks had rails on the sides of the flatbed and a gate along the back. Each truck was packed with women. It was standing room only. The women were coming and going from the factories where they earned just enough money to get by but not enough to get ahead. These textile factories produced clothes that would be shipped to our stores in America. Watching truck after truck file past my car window, I realized the cheap clothes I buy at home are made by these women who work in substandard conditions. In order for me to save a few dollars on a T-shirt, they were eking out a living.

Systems and structures. No one is innocent. All of us are complicit in our sin that impacts the whole world.

When confronted with the reality of systemic sin, we often defend ourselves by comparing our sin: "*I'm* not racist, but my uncle sure is." "I may be materialistic, but I work hard for what I have—unlike those who mooch free cell phones from the government." This doesn't magically eradicate the impact of our sin, but it does allow us to ignore our impact on the world by focusing attention on the sins of others. But this is a fool's game. All sin joins together to create, support, and perpetuate systems of injustice.

Those who best see and understand unjust systems are those whose necks are under the boots of oppression. We who benefit from sinful systems cannot clearly see them; we are blinded by an unconscious desire to have the status quo that we benefit from continue. And so we shut ourselves off to empathy. We refuse to listen. We go for the simple cause-and-effect solutions. We blame it all on poor choices. Maybe we even disregard the idea of systemic sin altogether.

Imagine telling someone about your pain, only to have them tell you it is imaginary. How frustrated would you be? How hurtful would that be?

Empathy begins with listening. Like our God who heard the cries of the Israelites while they suffered under Pharaoh's unjust brick quotas,[8] we need to hear the cries of our neighbors. Like our God who promises restorative justice and promises to right what's wrong, we need to be committed to justice. It's not enough just to listen; we must believe what our neighbors are telling us about injustice. Believing them is the first step to acting on their behalf. Episcopal priest and theologian Fleming Rutledge says it best:

> If, when we see an injustice, our blood does not boil at some point, we have not yet understood the depths of God. It depends, though, on what outrages us. To be outraged on behalf of oneself or one's group alone is to be human, but it is not to participate in Christ. To be outraged and to take action on behalf of the voiceless and oppressed, however, is to do the work of God.[9]

Shouldn't hearing about disproportionate numbers of unarmed black men being subjected to police brutality outrage those of us who believe in the value of every human life? What about hearing that one in six Americans struggles with hunger? Is outrage and action the work of God? Is it the work of God to take action for the voiceless children who did not choose to come to our country and who may be deported to a land they've never been to? Perhaps the work of God takes action for those oppressed by mountains of unpaid health care bills? Even if none of these things seem to affect us directly, maybe we *should* be outraged because God is outraged at injustice.

The action taken by God on behalf of the voiceless and

oppressed is to fully identify with their experience under an oppressive system. The Son of God was killed by a national system of punishment. The cross that liberates us was the cross that promised Roman citizens law and order. The cross that killed our Savior was a tool of the *Pax Romana*—the Peace of Rome. Those who were oppressed by Rome knew the cross well, and God revealed himself and his love in that place.

Elie Wiesel, a Jewish writer who lived through the horrors of Nazi concentration camps, records a moment when the Nazis hung three Jews, one of whom was a young child. The hanging commenced, and the men died quickly. But the young child, too light to quickly expedite his own death, hung at the end of the rope for a hellish amount of time. Wiesel records this:

> And so he remained for more than half an hour, lingering between life and death, writhing before our eyes. And we were forced to look at him at close range. He was still alive when I passed him. His tongue was still red, his eyes not yet extinguished.
>
> Behind me, I heard the same man asking:
> "For God's sake, where is God?"
> And from within me, I heard a voice answer:
> "Where He is? This is where—hanging here from this gallows."[10]

God is on the gallows. God is on the lynching tree. God is in the Palestinian ghetto. God is on the trail of tears. God is with every person who suffers. God is with us. This is why Christ suffered: to enter the entirety of the human experience. To redeem it from the inside out. To show so much love for humanity, and for the suffering that is such a part of that humanity, that he entered into it.

God is found, then, not by avoiding suffering but by pushing into it. If God seems far-off, then go to those who are suffering. God often seems far-off as we sit in our self-made, backyard Edens, protected from the suffering world.

Which leaves me wondering: *How does my desire for a comfortable and pain-free life contribute to the suffering of others? What do I not see about the systems and structures that impede another's flourishing? What is the impact of my inaction? Am I as empathetic as I want to believe I am?*

God desires that each person will flourish. "Be fruitful and increase in number" is another way to say, "May your family flourish."[11] The picture of every person sitting "under their own vine and under their own fig tree," with nothing to make them afraid, is a portrait of plenty and comfort.[12] Jesus gets in on the game by saying that he came so we "may have life, and have it to the full."[13] The flourishing of humanity is a core tenet of the shalom of God. Where flourishing is impeded, suffering is present. And to that place the justice of God is coming.

■　■　■

Back to Rudina's question: "What do you think we Palestinians deserve?"

I looked at Ludra and lost all my words—not an experience I'm used to. Typically, when I'm asked a question, my response comes quickly.

*What do Palestinians deserve?*

I knew what I believed about individuals. Individuals deserve to know that God sees them as worthy. But what do you say about a whole group of people? What do Palestinians living behind a wall deserve? What do African Americans whose families were ripped apart, who were sold as fodder to keep the American economy booming—what do they deserve? What do LGBTQ individuals who have been stigmatized and blamed for natural disasters deserve?

I didn't know what to say.

My three days on the West Bank had flipped my worldview upside down. I, like most Americans, had long accepted the idea that Israel was our friend and Palestine was our enemy. By default, that meant that Israelis were good and Palestinians were bad. Israelis deserved American support; Palestinians did not. But all of this had been muddied by a few days of getting to know the actual people.

This was not what I expected from my trip to the Holy Land. I expected to be overcome by what my missionary friend calls "the fifth gospel." The fifth gospel is the land. This is the land where the *Logos* of God took on flesh and walked. The land bears witness to the incarnation of God in Jesus of Nazareth in a way that even the text cannot. When you see the land and smell the air, when you walk the Temple Mount, stand in Caiaphas's palace, walk the road down the Mount of Olives into the Kidron Valley, and kneel in Gethsemane, something clicks. All of the sermons, all of the Bible studies, every flannelgraph Sunday school lesson I sat through, became tangible.

Psalm 50:2 reads, "From Zion, perfect in beauty, God shines forth." Had you asked me before I arrived in Jerusalem what I expected from the trip, that's what I would have said. I expected God to shine forth.

On the third day of our trip, that expectation met reality. We got into our van and went to East Jerusalem. We crossed an imaginary line drawn on a map by politicians in 1949, and instantly the road was filled with cracks and potholes. The edges of the road crumbled like stale crackers. Trash was scattered across the sides of the hill. Rooftops were adorned with large water tanks to keep taps flowing in houses and apartments when the city water was randomly turned off. We visited people who lived in fear that their homes would be demolished. We stood on the shattered remains of a family's hopes and dreams, the rubble and rebar of their home littering the sidewalk. A family that wanted exactly what I wanted from life—dinner together without worrying that my home would be unjustly taken from us, opportunities for my children to flourish, rooms to celebrate birthdays in, holidays filled with joy. Standing on the broken concrete, I saw the boot standing on the necks of these people.

The juxtaposition of West Jerusalem and East Jerusalem jarred my assumptions about the land.

Then on the third day, we saw the wall.

The wall dividing Israel from Palestine is protection for the Israelis and a prison for the Palestinians. It separates the right people from the wrong people. It separates family from family, friend from friend, haves and have-nots, rich and poor, deserving and undeserving, and people from hope. It cuts up the land, casting a long shadow across the beautiful face of Zion.

*From Zion, perfect in beauty, God shines forth?*

But beauty *was* shining forth. Staying with Jairus and Rudina and meeting their family, I saw so much beauty in the shadows of Zion. Beauty that was coming from people I had long believed to be bad. People who used to fit into a neat and clean categorization—Palestinians and Jews, evil and good, victim and villain, people to listen to and people to ignore.

Placing people into neat categories is easy in the absence of relationship. Relationship confuses the endeavor.

It's hard to think someone is bad when you dance in their living room with their family.

It's hard to think someone is evil when they will not let you out of the house without graciously giving you their scarf.

It's hard to think someone is a villain when they open their home to you.

It's hard to think someone is heinous when you sit and listen to their story and hear about only heartache, pain, and difficulty.

What do Palestinians deserve? I looked back at Rudina; I looked intently into her eyes. Her eyes said so much more than her question. Her eyes told me of the fear she lived with. Fear that her husband could, at any time and for any reason, be arrested as he crossed checkpoints for work. Fear that one of those bullets would find a family member instead of a wall. Anger that she was treated like a caged animal behind the wall around her country. Despair that the world she knows will not be different for Ludra.

My heart broke. "To live in peace," I said.

Tears filled her eyes. Rudina looked back at the floor and then at her daughter in my arms.

"Why doesn't the rest of the world think that?" she whispered.

For so long, my thoughts about Israelis and Palestinians were shaped about who deserved what. Palestinians deserved living behind the wall in a state-sanctioned prison because they couldn't control their people. Because they threatened the Israelis, who, after the horrific evil they've endured, deserve to have a land of their own. But looking at Rudina and holding

Ludra and seeing them as people changed everything. I was overcome with empathy.

It became clear to me. Jairus and Rudina did not deserve this. Palestinians didn't deserve this. Those whose flourishing is hampered by systemic injustice do not deserve the suffering they experience, the cruel shame of being blamed for their plight, and the damning isolation of not being believed. Jesus died for them and declared them worthy of his love. Jesus himself says that he came so all humans might have an abundant life. In other words, Jesus came so we could flourish.[14] He came so we could experience shalom—even when life is more than we can handle.

# CHAPTER 8

# BAPTISM, CROSSES, AND NEW CREATION

## *More Grace Than You Can Handle*

> The sound can only be described in other terms, mostly as mirth—the holy laughter of a God who seizes everything wrong and assures that it all turns out right ... there all the time, but never heard unless it's attended to. I hadn't been silent enough. I hadn't learned to wait. It was the sound of my name in God's mouth, the word that I was created and chosen to be, the part that I have been given in the chorus to shape into song.
>
> Harold Fickett, *The Holy Fool*

Sarah was shouting into the phone. "What! How does that happen? What!"

I sprinted up the stairs. A streak of panic shot through my body. Was it all falling apart again?

Three hours earlier, we had received the phone call we waited 1,802 days for—the child who would join our family was being born. We sent our son off to school. We rushed around the house, scrambling to get everything ready for the quick trip to Florida: pack, call the car rental company, call my mom to come and stay with Luke. We were a joy-filled whirlwind of activity. Then the phone rang again, and now Sarah was shouting.

I found her in the hallway. I only had to look at her face to see that things weren't falling apart. Her eyes were wide and dancing. Her mouth was wide open with surprise and joy. Her hands were flailing wildly.

I pieced together what happened from Sarah's half of the conversation. The baby had been born. Mother was doing well. Baby was healthy. A head full of hair.

And a *girl*.

This is what had Sarah hollering in a way that was difficult to decipher. Two ultrasounds with two different technicians had earlier confirmed that the child was going to be a boy. I'm not a doctor. I'm not a technician. But I do watch my fair share of TV, so I'm trained in looking at a screen. I'm confident in saying that seeing something that isn't there—*twice*—isn't normal. Apparently, ultrasounds aren't 100 percent accurate. But usually the mistake goes the other way—not seeing something that should be seen. Rarely is something seen that isn't there.

But the gender of the child isn't the point. Joy was exploding in our house. It was as though fireworks and music accompanied everything we did. We were like children laughing on Christmas morning as our long-held anticipation was realized. Newlyweds smashing cake into each other's faces had nothing on us. Two and a half years of wondering and wandering and waiting—and now the journey had a destination. Florida. I've never loved visiting Florida. The muggy heat, flat landscape, and warm-weather-seeking mass of humanity make it an undesirable destination. But on that day, Florida seemed like Eden. We couldn't get there fast enough.

A name! We hadn't even begun to think about girl names because everyone was convinced it was a boy. We'd have to take on that task in the car. Sarah had to make a quick trip to the store and buy some girl clothes. Every task we had to accomplish made us giddy. We would get to name a girl!

When Luke returned from school, the rental van had been packed, my mom was at our house, and we were ready to go. We just needed to let Luke in on the surprise. We sat him down at the kitchen table.

"Remember how we said your brother was going to be born today?"

"Yes."

"Well, the baby was born, but it wasn't a boy. It was a girl. You're going to have a sister! How do you feel about that?"

He paused for just a moment as the information settled into his five-year-old brain. And then he said what we all were feeling.

"I don't care. I just wanted a brother or a sister." Which is true. Over the past two and a half years, I heard him pray countless times for the baby who would come live with us. My heart broke every time he asked when his brother or sister would come live with us. He really didn't care if it was a boy or girl. His prayer was being answered. He was going to be a big brother.

Then he added, "Actually, I kind of wanted a sister."

We laughed and hugged. What else do you do in these moments? It's impossible to stay composed. And you wouldn't want to. Containing the overflow of emotions would cheapen the wonder and beauty. Emotions are a gift of God. Like the stars in the nighttime sky, they help us navigate the human experience, pointing the way to our true self and to where we need God. When suffering and pain are our lot, we enter fully into the grieving because that is what it means to be human. When joy and laughter come our way, we enter fully into the jubilation because that is what it means to be human. Embrace the experience. It's the only way to truly live.

That day, we were drinking undiluted joy. It watered the cracks that appeared over the landscape of our parched faith. Like a mountain snow melting in the warm spring sun and rushing to the dry valley below, joy spilled into every water-hungry crevice of our lives. Our excitement was palpable, like the buzz in the sanctuary before a bride enters the room.

We kissed Luke good-bye, left final instructions with my mom, and climbed into our van.

I looked over at Sarah and smiled for the thousandth time that day.

Tomorrow we would meet our daughter.

■ ■ ■

I can't help but wonder if our joy would have tasted as sweet had we not experienced the infertility, the ectopic pregnancy, the anxiety attacks. While the troubles and waiting seemed too much to handle, they primed our hunger for restoration. Just as the mountaintop doesn't seem as grand without the valley, I wonder if our elation wouldn't have been as overwhelming without the pain.

Psalm 126 is one of the Songs of Ascent. Required to pilgrimage to Jerusalem three times a year for the Passover, the Festival of Weeks, and the Festival of Booths, Jews would sing Psalms 120–134 as they prepared to be in the presence of the Lord. Psalm 126 reminds the people of their return from exile. For seventy years, the people of God were held captive by the Babylonians, and now the Lord was bringing them home.

As they journeyed to Jerusalem, they sang a song encapsulating the human experience:

> When the LORD restored the fortunes of Zion,
>> we were like those who dreamed.
>
> Our mouths were filled with laughter,
>> our tongues with songs of joy.
>
> Then it was said among the nations,
>> "The LORD has done great things for them."
>
> The LORD has done great things for us,
>> and we are filled with joy.
>
> Restore our fortunes, LORD,
>> like streams in the Negev.
>
> Those who sow with tears
>> will reap with songs of joy.
>
> Those who go out weeping,
>> carrying seed to sow,
>
> will return with songs of joy,
>> carrying sheaves with them.

To suffer is to be held captive by our circumstances. It is to be chained to pain. It is to be paralyzed by confusion. Suffering is an inescapable, chaotic darkness. And so, when the light shines in the darkness and our eyes begin to perceive a path forward, we are like captives being set free. Joy returns.

In the last stanza of the psalm, the psalmist makes an interesting connection between suffering and joy:

> Those who sow with tears
>> will reap with songs of joy.

> Those who go out weeping,
>     carrying seed to sow,
> will return with songs of joy,
>     carrying sheaves with them."[1]

This is an inversion of the karmic thinking that accompanies suffering. You don't reap what you sow. You don't get what you deserve. Those who sow sorrow will reap joy. Blessed are those who mourn, for they will be comforted. This is gospel.

And yet despite being set free and knowing joy, the psalmist prays, "Restore our fortunes."[2] The journey home was like a dream, but when the people of God arrived, they didn't find the Jerusalem they remembered. There were no homes. The city walls lay in ruins. The temple was destroyed. Fields and vineyards had grown wild after seventy years of neglect. Rebuilding was not going to be easy. As pastor and professor Stan Mast says about the returning Israelites, "They were out of hell, but they weren't in heaven yet."[3]

Life on earth isn't hell, but neither is it heaven. It is a mix of good and bad, beautiful and ugly, joy and sorrow, laughter and tears. You rejoice that you have a job now, but your company could be planning layoffs in the future. You feel relief that the marital conflict that rocked you has subsided, but you still feel shaken about the future. Parenting has been fun, but the dreaded teen years are around the corner and you're feeling anxious about the new pressures your kids will face. We are always in between, perpetually on the journey from exile to Zion, from hell to heaven.

Joy doesn't erase the pain of the journey. Our elation didn't erase the scars brought about by our experiences. I harbored a belief that, over time or with God's intervention, our experiences of suffering wouldn't leave significant marks on our lives. I've long resisted letting the negative experiences shape me. Bolstered by a strong sense of American triumphalism and the giftedness to make the best of my circumstances, I wanted to conquer my pain and suffering and render it insignificant. But it doesn't work that way. Try as we might, all our experiences form us.

Joy doesn't erase the pain, but it does strengthen us for the journey.

■ ■ ■

Most of us want a cure for our pain. We want something that will make the circumstance that brought the pain fixed. It could be an explanation, but often that's not enough. Explanations only bring a modicum of relief. We prefer the situation to be fixed—or maybe for everything to go back to the way it was. We want our loved one back. We want the security and stability we once had to be returned. We want the naiveté we once had to be restored.

But God doesn't work like that. God doesn't just offer a cure. God brings wholeness. Jesus didn't stop Peter from disowning him, but he did restore him. Jesus didn't end Mary's pain as she watched her son die, but he did see that she was cared for. Salvation is being saved both from something and to something. Jesus is saving us from death and to wholeness.

Jesus himself wasn't without his scars. We don't just grow from our experiences; we grow *into* our experiences. When we walk through the dark valleys of the shadow of death and come out on the other side, we don't forget the journey. It stays with us. Our bodies carry the signs of the rocks we've climbed over.

Our emotions know the valleys of the experiences. Our minds register that we are in a new place. When Jesus walked out of the tomb after three days, his body still told the story of the nails in his hands and the spear in his side. We will carry the scars we've accumulated on the journey for the rest of our lives.

In this, our pain and loss become a part of us. They shape us. It's not just that we will never be the same after them; it's that we *can't* be the same.

The writer of Hebrews says that "Son though he was, [Jesus] learned obedience from what he suffered and, once made perfect, he became the source of eternal salvation for all who obey him and was designated by God to be high priest in the order of Melchizedek."[4] That Jesus was "made perfect" after he suffered has mystified me. I was taught that Jesus was perfect from the beginning. In him was no sin. Ever. Therefore he had no need to be made perfect, and yet, according to the text, he not only was made perfect, but suffering was required in that process.

It's necessary to understand the idea of "perfect" as it is used in the Bible. *Perfect* can mean "never missing the mark." But it can also mean "wholeness," "completion," or "fulfillment." When Jesus was "made perfect," it is in this second sense. Agonizing in Gethsemane as blood dripped from his pores, he remained obedient and fulfilled his work on earth. He completed his baptismal call as the Son of God who would be the Suffering Servant.

In Matthew 5:48, Jesus tells us to "be perfect, therefore, as your heavenly Father is perfect." If Jesus is calling us to a sinless life, we will never be able to obey this command (and it is a command). But if Jesus is calling us to be whole and fulfill our calling, then in Christ we can. Baptized into Christ, we carry the death of Christ in our bodies and find ourselves ushered into a faith of paradoxes: in order to be first, we must be last; in order to live, we must die; in order to be whole, we must be broken.

Unfortunately, this means that if Jesus learned perfection or wholeness through suffering, it's likely we will too.

Our confidence is rooted in the perfection Jesus attained in suffering. Our hopeful future is brought about by the life, death, and resurrection of Christ. In Christ, God took on flesh and became human in the grandest display of sacrificial love. In the person of Jesus, God embodied the complete human experience—birth through death. Trace our Christian hope back to its genesis, beyond the resurrection, and you find a death. The Life we celebrate is the one that was glorified through death on a cross. As missionary and theologian Lesslie Newbigin wrote, "There is no Christian hope except that which is born at the resurrection out of the darkness and travail of being crucified with Christ. Those who do not know that defeat do not know that hope."[5] Darkness precedes dawn. Death comes before resurrection.

As Christians, we ought to speak openly and honestly about suffering and death because we meet them on the road to resurrection. Death and resurrection are, in Christ, intimately connected. When we speak of death, we cannot help but hear resurrection. We embrace suffering and death, not in some stoic act of resignation about our fate in the world. Rather, we face death because it is the only way to resurrection. And we do so with confidence because Jesus descended into death. God's grace is the reason for our defiant hope in the face of death. And where there is hope, joy is possible.

And yet we must be careful not to think that God causes all of our suffering. The impulse to definitively declare God's intent for suffering is driven by an anxious response to an uncertain world. But if there is a reason for suffering, it is not ours to know. Nor, I think, would it be helpful.

We wrongly look for comfort in sanitized explanations. Even if these explanations are accurate, they do not console us. Explaining to me why God had to allow us to experience infertility and an ectopic pregnancy would provide as much comfort to me as giving a child suffering from leukemia a detailed medical explanation for why he or she needs to have a painful bone marrow transplant. In that moment, all the child wants is the experience of their parents comforting them. We may say we want the explanation from God, but what we want is the firsthand knowledge that God is with us. There is no satisfying answer to our suffering—only a satisfying response: God with us.

This is why theologian C. S. Song wrote these words:

The suffering of Jesus the messiah has removed all human barriers. It makes God available to human beings and enables them to be part of the divine mystery of salvation. The depths of God's suffering ought to be the place where all persons, despite their different backgrounds and traditions, can recognize one another as fellow pilgrims in need of God's saving power . . . To be human is to suffer, and God knows that. That is why God suffers too. Suffering is where God and human beings meet. It is the one place where all persons—kings, priests, paupers, and prostitutes—recognize themselves as frail and transient human beings in need of God's saving love. Suffering brings us closer to God and God closer to us. Suffering, despite all its inhumanity and cruelty, paradoxically enables humans to long for humanity, find it, treasure it, and defend it with all their might.[6]

Both the Nicene Creed and the Apostles' Creed, which are the cornerstones of confessional Christianity, note only one thing about the life of Jesus: he suffered.[7] The creeds don't talk about Jesus laughing with friends, celebrating at a wedding, playing with children, sharing in the joy of the human experience. The focus of Jesus' humanity for the creeds is that he suffered.

In our suffering, we find God. In Christ, God meets us in suffering not simply to comfort us. God in Christ identifies with human sorrow, grief, and suffering in order to redeem the full human experience. God's sovereignty promises that every tear will be wiped from every eye, that every injustice will be corrected, that the oppressed will be set free, that oppressors will face justice. And somehow, in the mystery of it all, God will bring wholeness to those he redeems.

As the psalmist notes, "Weeping may tarry for the night, but joy comes with the morning."[8]

God meets us in suffering. Perhaps we can also say that joy comes through mourning.

■ ■ ■

Night was beginning to fall as we sped through the Georgia pines along I-65. The setting sun painted the horizon with pinks and oranges. The evening light highlighted the reddish-brown pine needles that covered the hills that the road followed. The tall pines lining the interstate beckoned travelers to slow their cars to the speed of a Southern drawl. Signs invited weary road warriors to take one of the plentiful exits and "enjoy a tall glass of sweet tea." "Have some BBQ." "Eat a peach." Tempting as the invitations may have been and stiff as our joints were from being in the car all day, we weren't stopping. Southern hospitality would have to be enjoyed another time.

We were getting closer to our daughter. The anticipation was uncomfortable, like a heavy blanket on a summer night. The closer we got, the quieter we became. Somewhere between Nashville and Georgia, we became present to a sobering reality: our joy exists because of another's grief.

How do you rejoice when another is mourning?

Adoption is an imperfect solution to an unfortunate set of circumstances. We weren't unaware of how difficult adoption is for birth mothers, but now we felt it viscerally. Especially Sarah. Having carried one child, she couldn't imagine feeling a baby grow inside her, experiencing those tiny butterfly flutters transform into a child's knee that jutted out of her tummy, and then being unable to watch that child grow up. She couldn't fathom becoming intimate with the little one's every movement in her womb and not getting to know her personality. She couldn't bear the thought of cradling that child and then entrusting her care to a stranger.

How does a mother walk out of a hospital without her child? No explanation makes sense except one: love. When people talk about the choice that birth mothers make, they often say something like, "They gave up their child for adoption." But that sounds like she gave up being a mother or, worse yet, gave up on her child. Birth mothers do not give up being mothers or give up on their children; they choose adoption because, like any mother who makes a thousand choices a day out of love for her children, she believes this is the best choice for her child. It is beyond difficult. It is heartbreaking. But it is founded on love.

As we imagined going to the hospital to meet our daughter,

we also imagined a broken mother leaving without her daughter. Our hearts would swell; another's heart would be crushed. Our faces would be awash with tears of joy; another's face would be awash with tears of sadness. We would joyfully be awake at night giving bottles and changing diapers; another would lie awake in grief.

Mile marker after mile marker, we closed in on this reality. I looked over at Sarah. She was staring out the window, tears trickling down her face. I reached over and took her hand.

"You okay?"

"I just can't stop thinking about her birth mother. How can I be both joyful and excited for us and heartbroken for her?"

I was silent.

I've learned to be comfortable when I don't have an answer.

■　■　■

Our stories never exist in isolation. The characters that come and go within our stories have their own stories. There are times when our stories converge with other humans and we celebrate standing side by side—cheering at a football game, gathering in a park for the Fourth of July, singing carols in church on Christmas Eve. At other times, we grieve together—gathered around our televisions on 9/11, collectively mourning the death of a beloved member of our community, standing at the scene of a horrific car accident. And at still other times, the range of emotions coexist in a single scene. Each person we encounter is on a pilgrimage between hell and heaven and we have no idea what role we will play in their story or what role they will play in ours.

There's a concept in mathematics known as fractals. Without

getting too far into the weeds with a definition, fractals are self-repeating patterns. Imagine a picture of hundreds of triangles within triangles. Zoom in one aspect of the triangle, and you find the same pattern as the larger picture; the repeating pattern allows you to zoom in infinitely and never find the end to the pattern.

There are mathematical equations that, when graphed, produce these repeating patterns. Often the mathematical equations producing fractal graphs are represented in nature. Picture a fern leaf. The entire leaf is made up of what looks to be smaller leaves. These smaller leaves are made up of still smaller leaves. Barnsley's Fern formula mathematically recreates the phenomenon.

Romanesco broccoli, a variant of cauliflower that looks like it was pulled from an overly pixelated computer screen, is the ultimate natural fractal. It's cone-shaped florets fit the Fibonacci sequence or golden spiral pattern perfectly. Break off a floret from the main head and you end up with a miniversion of the broccoli. You can continue to break off smaller and smaller pieces to get smaller and smaller versions of the broccoli because the pattern repeats over and over. Salt flats, branching trees, mountain ranges, and some shells contain naturally occurring repeating patterns.

What if suffering is a fractal experience of every human being?[9] I've told our story of suffering from the center, first-person narrative. Within our story of suffering and joy is the story of a young mother filled with grief as she made a heart-shattering decision to place her daughter with an adoptive family.[10] She must tell her story of suffering and joy. Her story will likely contain tears, anger, and frustration, just as they were present in our story. I don't know if she has faith, but if she does, my guess is that at some point, she will cry out to God from her wilderness. My hope in prayer is that, whether or not she has faith, God will be near her and will in some way redeem her and see to her flourishing. Within her story there will be others whose stories of suffering and joy will need to be told. And on and on and on it goes. Suffering is the common human experience.

Herein lies the learning: Our pain is an expression of a deeper, more real pain. Each of us has a story of the *tohu wabohu* being more than we can handle. For some it is personal; for others it is the story of a people oppressed by others. The circumstances of our suffering are all different, but they are all concrete. We suffer because we are hurt by people with names and faces; we suffer because our loved ones die too soon; we suffer because our humanity is not dignified because of the color of our skin. Our suffering is not theoretical. It is real. And so is our pain.

But underneath the unique plot points of our story is the human condition. We may wish to change the details of our lives. We may wish that our loved one didn't tragically die. Or that we didn't have to move back in with our parents because we lost our job and the bank foreclosed on our house. We may dream of a life where we never befriended that person so they never had the opportunity to betray us. It doesn't matter if we're able to change the events or substitute the characters of our life. The general plot would remain the same. We would still suffer. This is the human condition we all participate in. As Catholic priest and theologian Henri Nouwen wrote, "Your pain is the concrete way in which you participate in the pain of humanity."[11]

G. K. Chesterton once wrote, "We men and women are all in the same boat, upon a stormy sea. We owe to each other a terrible and tragic loyalty."[12] This is the condition God took on in the incarnation. The suffering of Jesus was the suffering of all humanity.[13]

God, in Jesus, entered into the fractal story of this broken world. Mary and Martha are grieving because their brother Lazarus has died. Jesus joins them in weeping and then raises Lazarus from the dead.[14] Zacchaeus has been ostracized by his community and suffers under the weight of his choice to collect taxes on behalf of Rome, and Jesus restores Zacchaeus's joy to him by taking on himself the ridicule of the religious leaders for dining with sinners, prostitutes, and tax collectors.[15] The disciples on the road to Emmaus despair over the death of Jesus, but Jesus breaks bread in their house and reveals his presence to them.[16] The gospel narratives are filled with stories of Jesus meeting people in their hell and moving them closer to heaven.

Our Christian, hopeful joy exists because of the suffering of another.

■　■　■

Sarah joined me in front of our church congregation with Luke and our newly adopted daughter, Evelyn—a name that means "wished-for child." With Evelyn placed in my arms, my family and I gathered around the baptismal font. Luke peered over the edge of the font to see the water. With my newly constituted family standing before the baptismal waters, I began to choke my way through the order for the sacrament.

Baptism is the sign and seal of God's promises to this covenant people.
In baptism God promises by grace alone:

to forgive our sins;

to adopt us into the Body of Christ, the Church;

to send the Holy Spirit daily to renew and cleanse us;

and to resurrect us to eternal life.

This promise is made visible in the waters of baptism.

I barely made it past the word *adopt*. Adoption is a metaphor often used by New Testament writers to help us make sense of our salvation. According to many passages, our salvation is our adoption into Jesus' family. Our heavenly Father adopts us as sons and daughters, and he wraps his robe around our shoulders, places his signet ring on our finger, and invites us into his house for a party he is throwing on our behalf. We are the prodigal who has returned. There we find our older brother Jesus, not outside the house, but inside. For he "is not ashamed to call [us] brothers and sisters."[17] This is our salvation.

The liturgy goes on:

For you Jesus Christ came into the world;

for you he died and for you he conquered death;

All this he did for you, little one,

though you know nothing of it as yet.

We love because God first loved us.

It was with many tears of joy that I reached into the font, cupped my hand, and sprinkled the water on my daughter's head in the name of the Father, and of the Son, and of the Holy Spirit. As the water dripped down around her eyes, it was a reminder that she—and all of us!—have a family to which we will belong forever. This is grace. Grace is that our heavenly Father will forever ensure our flourishing. That he will be present with us, no matter what we are facing. And that one day, the *tohu wabohu* of our lives will be brought to order. Immanuel. God with us. Baptized into the death and resurrection of Jesus, the incarnate God—who resurrected out of suffering—promises that we will rise out of our suffering into new life as well.

In baptism, we cannot avoid going under. We have to get into the water. In the water we remember that new life doesn't come by avoiding suffering, but by going through suffering. The baptismal waters prepare us for the full human experience. They strengthen us to embrace all that we finite beings might experience. The waters restore our lives, even while we simultaneously feel as though our lives are being depleted.

Our hope is not found in some magical incantation to make suffering disappear. Our hope is not found in a systematically satisfying explanation for our suffering. Our hope is not found by clinging with white knuckles to a stoic disposition while our hearts scream, "My God, my God, why have you forsaken me?"

Our hope is found in the waters where we are adopted as sons and daughters. The voice that spoke, "This is my son" over Jesus speaks over you and me. United to Christ, we become heirs to the inheritance that Jesus received. We are sons and daughters. Children of God. We belong to the God of creation, and he will not abandon us to the grave, to the chaos, to the pain, or to our tears.

The God of creation is the God of the new creation. The Spirit of God who hovered over the chaotic waters of the deep now hovers over us in our baptism. God is bringing order to our helter-skelter.

Theologian J. Todd Billings notes this about our adoption by the God of the new creation: "We have been adopted, but our new identity is coming to us from the future—an identity that is the Spirit's new creation."[18] Our baptism not only signifies but signs and seals God's promise to make us new as he is making all things new. Our situations, our pain, our suffering, our bodies, our wounds—all will be made new. We will become more human. More whole. More of our true selves as God establishes his presence with us forevermore. Whatever may be true about our suffering, God's presence with us is *truer still*. Restoration is coming.

As a family we've tasted some of that restoration. Holding my daughter over the waters of baptism was an undeniable sign of God's goodness. God's love is steadfast, enduring through the helter-skelter that we fear will overwhelm us.

The Hebrew word for this love is *hesed*. It's a difficult word to translate, but we know a few things about the word from context. First, *hesed* always involves an interpersonal relationship. Second, it does not denote a feeling for someone. Rather, it is a word about practical action on behalf of another. And third, *hesed* is enduring. It represents a commitment toward a person. This leads many to translate the word "loyal love."[19]

Baptism reminds us of God's loyal love for us and toward us. No matter what we've gone through. Regardless of whether we've come through the helter-skelter or whether we are still in its eye. We will be restored by the God who is with us and by his loyal love for us.

I felt that truth as I cupped the water and placed my hand on my daughter's head. We were being restored. Order was coming to the chaos. More meaning—not explanation—was given to our experience than I could ever have imagined.

To be clear, the adoption of our daughter wasn't our salvation. Her adoption didn't magically erase the pain or the questions.

She's not really the answer to our prayers. She's not the miracle we've been waiting on. She's not even our hearts' deepest desire. That's a yoke too heavy for her to bear. Our two and a half years of *tohu wabohu* taught us what we always knew: Jesus is the answer and the miracle and our deepest desire. Sunday school answers are sometimes the right answers to life's questions. Unfortunately, while we learn the answer in Sunday school, we don't really know the answer until we've walked through the fire. It's only then that our eyes see Jesus with us.

Nor does the adoption of our daughter mean we're saving her. Far from it. That's a significant difference in her adoption into our family and our adoption by God the Father in Jesus. She has become a Pyle, and we'll be with her in life when she's got questions and struggles and pain. One day, she'll tell a very different story about her adoption—one that will be emotionally complicated with loss, grief, and, I hope, gratitude and joy. We won't be able to answer all of her questions. We will only be with her. Which is all we can be for her. We cannot be with her and transform the pain and suffering she is sure to face. The comfort we can provide her is a mere shadow of the comfort that God can provide. For not only will her heavenly Father be with her in the helter-skelter, but God will redeem the helter-skelter. God is with us as God saves us. God is not distant from our pain, and neither is God overwhelmed by what overwhelms us. Resurrection teaches that God is never overwhelmed. God overcomes. That's our hope.

So we haven't saved our daughter, and she hasn't saved us. Instead, we've experienced the grace of Jesus that overcomes our chaos and creates something new. We've become family.

Sometimes the story of how God created our family is more than I can handle.

# ACKNOWLEDGMENTS

Writing this book was an exercise in sheer determination. First, I had to get past the voices telling me I wasn't a good writer; my pain wasn't as profound as others; the number of books on pain and suffering are legion; and sleeping would be time better spent. Second, I had to fight my calendar and to-do list more than I did for my first book. That led to the question, "What is wrong with me?" Which led back to the voices of point one. Third, every word had to be wrangled from my muse's stingy hands—if I even have a muse. I'm convinced writers made up the idea of muses so they have something to project their frustration on. Even if muses are real, *I* wrote this book and they were of no help whatsoever. No thanks for them.

I would like to thank the amazing congregation at Christ's Community Church. For ten years you've continued to call me pastor. More than that, you've let me grow into a pastor. You hired me fresh out of seminary, trusted the Holy Spirit to grow me up, and participated in that process. I'm beyond grateful for the opportunity to work out our salvation together.

Thank you to Marv and Carol Norman and Monty Beard for being willing to let your stories into the world. Thanks for entrusting me with them.

Thank you to my agent, Jenni Burke, for believing in me and this project. When things got tough and we wondered if this project would become a reality, you abandoned the role of agent and took on the role of friend. Navigating those spaces is what makes you so amazing at your job.

Thank you to my editor Carolyn McCready, who made this book better. A good editor is a good friend. They ask questions like, "Do you really mean this?" "Aren't you contradicting yourself?" And, of course, "What does this even mean?" It takes courage to ask those questions. If that wasn't enough, our conversation in Grand Rapids helped frame the second half of the book. I'm grateful you gave so much time and attention to the ideas and the words within these pages.

Thank you to Dirk Buursma for your wonderful attention to detail and encouragement in the editing process. To the other folks at Zondervan for believing in the project, designing the cover, working on marketing, and supporting the project in a myriad of ways—thank you.

Thank you to a whole host of amazing friends who encouraged me to write this book: Nish Weiseth, the sister I never had, for encouraging and reasoning with me as I waded into some of the more sensitive concepts and ideas; Jim Herrington and Trisha Taylor for reading early drafts of the first few chapters and affirming the necessity of doing this hard work; Seth Haines for helping me wrestle through titles and strategy and what it means to be a writer; Matthew Paul Turner for randomly checking in with me to ask how it was going; Matt Tebbe and Ben Sternke for our random buffet lunches; Matt Bays for your encouragement.

A special thank you to Jeff Chu. The amount of work you put into this book is astounding. When I think about your willingness to listen to me on the phone, respond to my texts, and then read and edit most of the chapters—it's overwhelming. I'm beyond grateful for you and your friendship.

To Evelyn's birth mother—I don't have words. Our joy is bound up with your grief. How can I express gratitude for that? We honor you regularly in our home.

Thank you to my family, who gave me the space and time to write the book. Thank you, Sarah, for being my constant companion. I'm in awe of your courage in letting this story be told. We went through the chaos together. We'll likely go through some more. Whatever we face, we'll make the journey together. I love you and our life together.

And to Immanuel—God with us. For that good news, gratitude overflows.

# NOTES

## Foreword

1. Elisabeth Kübler-Ross, *Death: The Final Stage of Growth* (New York: Simon & Schuster, 1986), 96.

## Introduction

1. Joseph P. Czarnecki, *Last Traces: The Lost Art of Auschwitz* (New York: Atheneum, 1989), 11.

## Chapter 1: More Than You Can Handle

1. See Psalm 34:18.
2. See Matthew 7:24–27.
3. "The Wise Man Built His House upon the Rock" (composer unknown).
4. C. S. Lewis, *Mere Christianity* (1943; repr., New York: Macmillan, 1960), 190.
5. Matthew 14:22–33; Mark 6:45–51; John 6:16–21.
6. Matthew 8:23–27; Mark 4:35–41; Luke 8:22–25.
7. See John 3:16.

## Chapter 2: Faith Enough to Doubt

1. Robert Huber, "Why Did the Schaibles Let Their Children Die?" www.phillymag.com/articles/schaibles-let-children-die/2/#coVhe3RQsCRwhejV.99.
2. Huber, "Why Did the Schaibles Let Their Children Die?"
3. This paragraph is based on the thoughts of Douglas John Hall. He points to the idea of cheap and costly hope in his book *God and Human Suffering: An Exercise in the Theology of the Cross* (Minneapolis: Augsburg, 1989), 28.
4. Fleming Rutledge, *The Crucifixion: Understanding the Death of Jesus Christ* (Grand Rapids: Eerdmans, 2015), xvii.
5. Jeremiah 17:5–6.
6. Jeremiah 17:7–8.

## Chapter 3: How Long, O Lord?

1. Job 30:20.
2. Proverbs 3:6.
3. Proverbs 4:26 NASB.
4. Proverbs 12:28 ESV.
5. Matthew 10:30.
6. Matthew 10:29.
7. Matthew 6:28–30.
8. J. Todd Billings, *Rejoicing in Lament: Wrestling with Incurable Cancer and Life in Christ* (Grand Rapids: Brazos, 2015), 58.
9. Revelation 21:3–4.
10. Douglas John Hall, *God and Human Suffering: An Exercise in the Theology of the Cross* (Minneapolis: Augsburg, 1989), 126.
11. Matthew 27:46.
12. Genesis 32:26.

13. Paul Tillich, *The Courage to Be* (New Haven, CN: Yale University Press, 1952), 39.

## Chapter 4: The Deepest Desire

1. I was first introduced to this idea in Douglas John Hall, *God and Human Suffering: An Exercise in the Theology of the Cross* (Minneapolis: Augsburg, 1989).
2. Hall, *God and Human Suffering*, 59.
3. Jeremiah 17:9.
4. Robert Farrar Capon, *Between Noon and Three: Romance, Law, and the Outrage of Grace* (Grand Rapids: Eerdmans, 1997), 74.
5. Ephesians 2:1.
6. Romans 6:23.
7. Romans 5:8.
8. Romans 8:38–39.
9. Galatians 6:7.
10. See Deuteronomy 28:4, 11; 30:9.
11. Romans 3:23.
12. Philippians 2:14–15.
13. Karl Barth, *Epistle to the Philippians* (Louisville, KY: Westminster John Knox, 2002), 77, emphasis original.
14. Philippians 2:15.
15. See Philippians 2:6–8.
16. John 3:16.
17. Philippians 2:12.

## Chapter 5: Doubting Our Doubts

1. Parker J. Palmer, *Let Your Life Speak: Listening for the Voice of Vocation* (San Francisco: Jossey-Bass, 2000), 97.

2. See Genesis 32:22–32.

3. Douglas John Hall, *God and Human Suffering: An Exercise in the Theology of the Cross* (Minneapolis: Augsburg, 1989), 80.

4. Job 1:1.

5. Kate Bowler's work centers on this idea; see her *Blessed: A History of the American Prosperity Gospel* (New York: Oxford University Press, 2013), and *Everything Happens for a Reason: And Other Lies I've Loved* (New York: Random House, 2018).

6. Eleonore Stump, *Wandering in the Darkness: Narrative and the Problem of Suffering* (Oxford: Oxford University Press, 2010), 207.

7. See Hebrews 11:1.

8. 1 Peter 5:7.

9. Luke 1:46–55 ESV.

10. Dallas Willard, *The Allure of Gentleness: Defending the Faith in the Manner of Jesus* (New York: HarperOne, 2015), 28.

11. David Bentley Hart, *The Doors of the Sea: Where Was God in the Tsunami?* (Grand Rapids: Eerdmans, 2005), 89.

**Chapter 6: How Beauty Blooms**

1. Genesis 12:1.

2. See Fleming Rutledge, *The Crucifixion: Understanding the Death of Jesus Christ* (Grand Rapids: Eerdmans, 2015), 262.

3. See Rutledge, *Crucifixion*, 263–66.

4. Genesis 12:2; 22:2.

5. Daniel 3:16–18.

6. Revelation 21:4.

7. I know this is atrocious English, but I also like it. There it is.

8. Genesis 2:23

9. Terence E. Fretheim, *Creation Untamed: The Bible, God, and Natural Disasters* (Grand Rapids: Baker, 2010), 14.

10. See Genesis 32:22–32.

11. See Philippians 2:8–9.

12. Douglas John Hall, *God and Human Suffering: An Exercise in the Theology of the Cross* (Minneapolis: Augsburg, 1989), 60.

13. Job 38:8.

14. Eleonore Stump, *Wandering in the Darkness: Narrative and the Problem of Suffering* (Oxford: Oxford University Press, 2010), 190.

15. I borrowed this example from Stump, *Wandering in the Darkness*, 225.

16. Stump, *Wandering in the Darkness*, 217.

17. Stump, *Wandering in the Darkness*, 217.

18. Job 42:7 ESV.

19. Job 42:5.

20. See Daniel 3.

21. Daniel 3:17–18.

22. Isaiah 53:3.

23. Colossians 1:15 NLT.

24. John 1:2–3.

25. See 2 Corinthians 8:9.

26. John 1:14.

27. Charles Spurgeon, "The Man of Sorrows: A Sermon Delivered on Lord's Day Morning, March 2, 1873," www .king-james-bible-study.com/sermons-by-spurgeon-library/ sermon-1099-the-man-of-sorrows-25401.

28. Ecclesiastes 7:2.

29. 1 Kings 8:12 ESV.

30. See Leviticus 16:11–14 and Hebrews 9:7 for evidence of this practice.
31. See Matthew 27:45–53.
32. See John 1:5.
33. Frederick Buechner, *Lion Country* (New York: Atheneum, 1971), 247.

### Chapter 7: Eyes Opened

1. See Job 2:13.
2. This idea was fully articulated by Dr. Martin Luther King Jr. when he said, "When white Americans tell the Negro to lift himself by his own bootstraps, they don't look over the legacy of slavery and segregation. I believe we ought to do all we can and seek to lift ourselves by our own bootstraps but it's a cruel jest to say to a bootless man that he ought to lift himself by his own bootstraps." This quote comes from a 1967 interview shared by NBC News on their Facebook page, www.facebook .com/NBCNews/videos/2505848169435198/?hc_ref=ARQy 0kok-xVM5vqCvgbORrihoIWsowiU80sbnxiuX0-mnm PLt4f3QY2mtAyd7O4BuxI.
3. Eleonore Stump, *Wandering in the Darkness: Narrative and the Problem of Suffering* (Oxford: Oxford University Press, 2010), 8.
4. Michelle Alexander writes, "People of all races use and sell illegal drugs at remarkably similar rates." She also notes that while the majority of drug users in America are white (because whites outnumber minorities), "three-fourths of all people imprisoned for drug offenses have been black or Latino" (*The New Jim Crow: Mass Incarceration in the Age of Colorblindness* [New York: New Press, 2010], 98–99).

5. According to a study in New Jersey, 15 percent of all drivers
   on the New Jersey Turnpike were racial minorities, yet
   42 percent of all stops and 73 percent of all arrests were
   of black motorists. This disparity exists despite evidence
   that blacks and whites break traffic laws at the same rate.
   A Maryland study found similar trends: 17 percent of
   drivers along a stretch of I-95 outside of Baltimore were
   black, yet 70 percent of traffic stops were of black drivers.
   On this, see Alexander, *The New Jim Crow*, 133.
6. Alexander, *The New Jim Crow*, 118, emphasis original.
7. Ephesians 6:12.
8. See Exodus 6:5.
9. Fleming Rutledge, *The Crucifixion: Understanding the
   Death of Jesus Christ* (Grand Rapids: Eerdmans, 2015), 143.
10. Elie Wiesel, *Night*, rev. ed. (1972; repr., New York: Hill and
    Wang, 2006), 65.
11. Genesis 1:28.
12. Micah 4:4.
13. See John 10:10.
14. It is not within the scope of this book to dissect what we
    mean when we say, "Jesus came so we could flourish." It's a
    statement that requires examination. Clearly, with his call
    to deny ourselves and take up our cross (see Matthew 16:24),
    Jesus is redefining culture's assumptions about flourishing.
    Some suffering—the suffering of self-denial, putting
    others' needs above ourselves, praying for one's enemies,
    or working for peace—results in flourishing. Flourishing
    doesn't equal comfort, tranquility, and a struggle-free
    existence. It means we live life as God intended it—fully
    human, fully alive.

## Chapter 8: Baptisms, Crosses, and New Creation

1. Psalm 126:5–6.
2. Psalm 126:4.
3. Stan Mast, "The Lectionary Psalms: Psalm 126," Center for Excellence in Preaching, http://cep.calvinseminary.edu/sermon-starters/lent-5c/?type=the_lectionary_psalms.
4. Hebrews 5:8–10.
5. Lesslie Newbigin, *Missions Under the Cross*, ed. Norman Goodall (London: Edinburgh House, 1953), 109.
6. C. S. Song, *The Compassionate God: An Exercise in the Theology of Transposition* (Maryknoll, NY: Orbis, 1982), 115.
7. See Fleming Rutledge, *The Crucifixion: Understanding the Death of Jesus Christ* (Grand Rapids: Eerdmans, 2015), 56.
8. Psalm 30:5 ESV.
9. I'm indebted to Eleanor Stump's thoughts about the fractal nature of suffering. In *Wandering in the Darkness* (Oxford: Oxford University Press, 2010), 220–22, she goes into much greater detail than I can here.
10. I refuse to say "gave up for adoption." Mothers and fathers do not "give up" on their children when they enter the adoption process. The reason they take on the grief and pain of placing their child with another family is that they haven't given up on that child; they have all the hope, all the dreams, all the expectations, every parent does. They simply have experienced a set of circumstances that makes it difficult or impossible to be the one who parents their child.
11. Henri J. Nouwen, *The Inner Voice of Love* (New York: Doubleday, 1998), 103.
12. G. K. Chesterton, *All Things Considered* (New York: Lane, 1909), 290.

13. See Nouwen, *Inner Voice of Love*, 104.

14. See John 11.

15. See Luke 19:1–10.

16. See Luke 24:13–35.

17. Hebrews 2:11.

18. J. Todd Billings, *Union with Christ: Reframing Theology and Ministry for the Church* (Grand Rapids: Baker, 2011), 31.

19. Will Kynes, "God's Grace in the Old Testament: Considering the *Hesed* of the Lord," www.cslewisinstitute .org/webfm_send/430.

# Man Enough

## How Jesus Redefines Manhood

*Nate Pyle*

*Man Enough* challenges the idea that there's one way to be a man. The masculinity that pervades our church and culture often demands that men conform to a macho ideal, leaving many men feeling ashamed that they're not living up to God's plan for them. Nate Pyle uses his own story of not feeling "man enough," as well as providing sociological and historical reflections, to help men see that manhood isn't about what you do, but it's about who you are. It's not about the size of your paycheck, your athletic ability, or your competitive spirit. You don't have to fit any masculine stereotype to be a real man.

In our culture and churches, quieter and more thoughtful or compassionate personalities, as well as stay-at-home dads, are often looked down on. Sermons, conferences, and publications often focus on helping men become "real men." This pressure to have one's manhood validated is antithetical to gospel living and negatively affects how men relate to each other, to women and children, and to God.

*Man Enough* roots men in the gospel, examines biblical examples of masculinity that challenge the idea of a singular type of man, and ultimately encourages men to conform to the image of Jesus—freeing men up to be who they were created to be: a son of God who uniquely bears his image.

Available in stores and online!